Strengthening Our Faith One Moment at a Time

Feed your moment!

BY CHRISTINE THERESE SCHMIDT

I.H.S. Publishers
St. Louis, MO ~ Orange, CA

Copyright © 2011 Christine Schmidt.

All rights reserved.

No part of this book may be used or reproduced by any means, graphic, electronic, or mechanical, including photocopying, recording, taping or by any information storage retrieval system without the written permission of the publisher.

I.H.S. Publishers
P.O.Box 2983
Orange, Ca 92859
714-744-0336

Scripture texts in this work are taken from the New American Bible with Revised New Testament and Revised Psalms © 1991, 1986, 1970 Confraternity of Christian Doctrine, Washington, D.C., and are used by permission of the copyright owner. All Rights Reserved. No part of the New American Bible may be reproduced in any form without permission in writing from the copyright owner.

Cover and Layout Design by Trese Gloriod
Cover Photo by Lorraine Swanson | Dreamstime.com

Printed in the United States of America

ISBN: 978-0-6154-0505-6

In Memory of
Robert Duncan

An amazing father who loved me with all his heart and accepted me for who I was but always helped me strive for more.

A special mention to
Daniel Dunn

who has accepted my family into his own and has loved and cared for each of us.

Dedication

This book is most lovingly dedicated to my husband and best friend, Derek, whom I cherish and love beyond words, and to my children: Allyson, Morgan, Mackenzie, and Andrew. They provide me with more love than any one person deserves and support me daily in my faith journey as well as inspire me to be the best that I can be.

I thank my mom, Karen Dunn, for always seeing the potential which lies within me. Your support, encouragement and excitement has meant a great deal to me. You are a wonderful, caring mother and have always been one of my closest friends. I will forever be one of your greatest fans. I love you dearly.

Matt and Robyn, my dearest brother and sister, you each hold a very special and tender spot within my heart. I love you both dearly.

Sandy, my dear, sweet, mother-in-law, you are sure joy and love. Thank you for your friendship, love, and support. And Chuck, you have always loved me as a daughter. I am more than proud to be a part of your family.

I also wish to thank my dear friends for their continued support and for living faithful lives worth emulating, and who believed in me from the very beginning: Kelly, Kathleen, Shannon, Terri (my biggest fan!), and many, many more. You're the best anyone could ask for.

Thank you, Lu Cortese, for seeing a spark and walking with me on this new and exciting journey.

I thank our Almighty Father for the gift of faith He has blessed me with and for the courage to share that faith with those I care the deepest for.

Introduction

*D*o you ever feel like you're all alone? Or that no one quite understands where you are or where you've been? I've been there, too, and so have many other women just like you. We are the moms with full calendars, working women with demands and pressures that seem to reach beyond our abilities. We are daughters, wives, volunteers. One Truth remains: We are all children of God, an Almighty and loving Father.

Whether we're in the car pool lane, the gym, nursing a sick child, running a board room, or rejoicing in the glory of a beautiful morning, our one true friend is always by our side.

The Word of God is our roadmap to a better life lived in grace. Within the following pages are reflections inspired by scripture and brought to life by real stories from a real woman just like you. The devotions are special and purposeful.

Following each devotion, a quote from a Catholic saint is provided to continue to bring His Word to life in a most meaningful way. As Catholics, we live by scripture, and who best to emulate but those deemed worthy of sainthood. By studying the teachings and philosophies of our ancestral brothers and sisters in Christ, we, too, can find our way. May these quotes enlighten you, entertain you, and touch your heart.

Those who were deemed holy saints by the Catholic Church went through several steps lasting decades, even centuries, to be canonized. These individuals did not apply to sainthood or seek it. In fact, these men and women were extremely humble and most charitable in their work for God. In most cases they redirected *all* compliments to God. Their modesty, generosity, sacrifice, and deep love for and faith in our God is admirable at the very least. Their works, healings and miracles have been verified. They have lived a life worthy of imitation. Because the church has confirmed that those we call saints are most certainly in heaven, we also ask them to pray for us—to intercede for us before the throne of God.

"Follow the Saints because those who follow them will become saints."

St. Pope Clement I

It is my most sincere prayer that you will find humor and enjoyment in reading about my adventures as well as be inspired to reflect on your own personal story. After reading each devotion, you can experience the closeness and the deep connection I feel every time I open my bible. I implore you to reflect on your own personal experience and how God has shown you the way. There is space at the back of the book for your journaling. With a new verse and a prayer to start your day, together we will experience life, love and the Word: one day at a time.

"What eye has not seen, and ear has not heard, and what has not entered the human heart, what God has prepared for those who love him." 1 Corinthians 2:9

God Bless you,

Christine

"For you had gone astray like sheep, but you have now returned to the shepherd and guardian of your souls." 1 Peter 2:25

Let me share something with you. On the island in my kitchen, I have a small tea light holder that reads, "Remember, the Lord is always there." I keep it lit whenever I am home. It helps to remind me that the Lord is always there, in my heart, in my home, in my life. Pretty bold for such a small tea light! I pray in front of it; I encourage my children to do the same. When the candle is not lit, they ask why.

Yesterday I woke up and something made me cranky. I received an email that just started my day off sour—and before my morning coffee! I lit the candle. I stared at it in contempt. I thought to myself, "I'll pray later." Every time I walked by the candle, I could feel it tugging at me! I could actually hear a whisper in my head, in my heart, in my soul. It was saying, "Come to me, and I will heal you. I will heal your mood. I will bless your day." And you know what? I actually said "NO. I want to feel this way. I want to hang on to this . . . just for a while."

All day long I felt as though I was treading water, spinning my wheels. I had emptiness in my day. I didn't read my scripture as usual. Boy, was I rebelling!

Have you ever made the conscious choice not to choose God? I haven't in a long time. It's like pushing away your best friend when he wants to be with you. How hurt the Lord must have been yesterday with my refusal. But you know what? He's always here for us, even when we turn away from Him.

I did pray to the Lord in the afternoon. Actually, before my husband walked in the door. I needed that peace before he came in. I needed the blessing on our home. And He was there for me! I was happy again. I was available for my family mentally, physically and emotionally. Thank you, Jesus!

This morning, I lit my little candle. I started my day the right way: in the Word of the Lord. And I prayed.

Dearest Heavenly Father, thank You for the many blessings You've bestowed on me. Thank You for my many friends and family. Thank You for watching over us all and keeping us safe in Your loving grace. Please continue to care for my friends and their families. Help them and all to remember to return to You, Oh Lord. You are the One. *Amen.*

"How often I failed in my duty to God, because I was not leaning on the strong pillar of prayer." St. Teresa of Avila

"I will bless the Lord at all times; praise shall be always in my mouth." Psalms 34:2

There is a very specific image that comes to mind when I read this passage. Picture if you will: The day is fresh and new, the dew still kissing the blades of grass. Now picture a child, maybe it's you or one of your children. With the sun streaming down from the heavens, you close your eyes and feel its warmth. In a spontaneous response, your arms rise outstretched from the sides of your body. You begin to run, feeling the wind against your face like the breath of Jesus Himself. Can you see yourself smiling? How happy and carefree you are.

You know it's very much like that when we walk in the light of Christ. When we seek His love and glorify Him, we can feel as though we're walking on sunshine. (You remember that song? I bet you're singing it right now!) No harm can come to us. We feel His warmth.

There are times when we get too busy to worship. Our egos get in the way of giving credit to the Lord for the blessings in our life. Often we think we can do it on our own.

Now picture that same child falling. Unexpectedly tripping on a stone or running too fast to keep up with his own feet.

As with a child falling who cries out for help and has his tears wiped dry and his scrapes bandaged, we, too, cry out for the

Lord in our hour of need. And as our Heavenly Father, He, too, dries our tears. He lights our path. He shows us His goodness.

*D*ear Lord, thank You for the love You have for me. Help me to remember to walk in Your light. Thank You for guiding me and for healing me. *A*men.

"It is the highest duty of religion to imitate Him whom you adore."

St. Augustine of Hippo

"But the Lord said to Samuel: "Do not judge from his appearance or from his lofty stature, because I have rejected him. Not as man sees does God see, because man sees the appearance but the Lord looks into his heart." 1 Samuel 16:7

*Y*ou know that woman at the gym with the perfect body, great hair, and beautiful smile? Or the mom in church with the cutest little kids and the handsome husband; her clothes are of the latest fashion, and a hair barely out of place?

How many times have we judged others based on their appearance alone? Have we assumed their life is perfect? Maybe we've thought, "They don't have a cross to bear. They're not like me."

Have we felt jealous or envious of their lives simply based on their appearance?

I wonder how many times I've been judged. How many times have you been judged?

We all have a story. We all have a cross to bear.

When you look on the outside you'll see one thing. But if you look closer, really getting to know someone, you'll see the tracks of their tears. You'll also see them the way our Father sees all of us. He sees our hearts.

10

𝒟earest Lord, help me to look beyond the outside appearance of others. Help me to see their heart, the way You see them. 𝒜men.

"If love dwells in you, you have no enemy on earth."

St. Ephraem the Syrian

"My help comes from the Lord, the maker of heaven and earth. God will not allow your foot to slip, your guardian does not sleep." Psalms 121:2–3

𝒯his past summer my great friend and I took the kids to the pumpkin patch. It was a warm, October day. The sun was high in the sky. The leaves had begun changing color, and you could hear a faint rustle in the wind. It was the sound of cornstalks coming from the maze.

Of course the kids ran ahead of us. In less than a minute all returned . . . but one.

My friend and the kids stayed at the entrance of the maze, and I went in after my little girl. At first I was walking—trying to peek in between the rows of corn. I was yelling her name. And then I'd listen. There was nothing but the sound of the wind and the corn.

My walk turned into a frantic run going in and out of the rows. Minutes turned into an hour in that maze. I was crying out her name at this point. I'd cry out for her and then listen. Now I could hear others yelling for her, too.

I was running in circles, asking, "Where could she be? Why isn't she answering?" I was thinking only about the bad things that could have happened. Worst of all was the thought of going home without her.

I recall hopelessly stopping and grabbing my knees. I cried to God, "Where is she? Please be with her Lord. Bring her back to me."

11

I kept thinking that if she were there she would answer me. Why wasn't she answering me?

This story has a happy ending. Thank God.

My daughter left that cornfield trying to find her own way out. She wandered to a gravel road outside of the maze, outside the boundaries of the farm. By the grace of God she was picked up by a good family who brought her back to the farm.

I have never been so thankful for anything in my life. I have no doubt that she was in God's care the entire time.

Have you ever felt so lost? And then, so found? Take comfort in knowing that your Father never sleeps. He is with you always.

*D*ear Lord, I take refuge in the knowledge that You are my guardian and keeper. No harm shall come to me.   *A*men.

"We shall steer safely through every storm, as long as our heart is right, our intention fervent, our courage steadfast, and our trust fixed in God."   St. Francis de Sales

"Ask of the Lord rain in the spring season! It is the Lord who makes the storm clouds, and sends men the pouring rain; for everyone, grassy fields." Zachariah 10:1

*M*MMM .... Do you smell it? It's the smell of dirt, slightly muddy. It's the aroma of fresh grass emerging from once frozen soil. On a fresh spring day you can almost hear the new buds popping like popcorn, just waiting for the warmth of the sun. They are swelling with new life—ready to show their glory. There's a warm breeze, just soft enough to make you close your eyes and smile. You take in a long, deep breath before slowly exhaling. Ahhh. The warm breath of spring.

Spring is a time for new life. Yes, there is the new life of the flowers and trees, and the critters that love to eat my flowers!

There's also a spring of new life within us, within our souls. It is a time for awakening. When we accept Jesus' law, we are like the new buds swelling with His love, ready to show our glory. We are called upon to be His plants of the field.

As is true with the emerging spring, our spring of new life is not so pretty at first. Like the left over leaves from fall and the pots of dead flowers neglected at the end of summer, our spring may be filled with regrets and sins that we've tried to forget about, pushing them out of the way for another day or another season.

Our sufferings in this life are not in vein. The Lord will not give us more than we can handle. He brings on the clouds only for us to ask Him to bring on the rain. To wash us clean and emerge from our old life and enter into a new life . . . in Him!

Thank You, O Lord, for all things, especially the clouds of our sufferings. We turn to You, O Lord, for Your grace and mercy. Be with us always. Spring Your new life into us!

Amen.

"First let a little love find entrance into their hearts, and the rest will follow."
St. Philip Neri

"Draw near to God, and He will draw near to you." James 4:8

One of my favorite movies is the one where a young girl is taken from her farm in Kansas to a far-away land. I first saw it at my grandma's house. Her name was Teresa, but her friends called her Tess. She pulled out the hide-a-bed in front of the television and went to the kitchen to make us some popcorn. This was the real stuff: kernels popping in oil over a black iron skillet, followed by melted butter and salt! MMM! That was before counting calories. But then, I was only seven!

In the movie, the girl finds herself in a far-off land on the other side of the rainbow. She encounters adventures, friendship,

magic and self-discovery. She hears of a wizard who can send her back home. Throughout her journey to the land of Oz, she picks up friends along the way who also need healing or fulfillment in some way. While many things are beautiful, some are also ugly and scary: much like our journey through this life.

Not long ago I did something to someone very close to me. It hurt this person. It was so uncharacteristic of me that not only was I hurt but I was so disappointed in myself. I was standing in the shower, numb from my self-inflicted broken heart. My eyes were swollen and chapped from crying, and I felt worthy of the pain I was feeling. I cried to God and asked why He let me do this? But was it really His fault? How dare I blame Him. It was at the same time I was asking, "Why," that I felt the urge to thank God, right in that moment. Although I was hurting, I thanked Him for the opportunity of teaching me a lesson: a lesson that I, too, can fall. I asked the Lord to forgive me and to bless me. He pointed me to scripture that helped heal me. My best friend forgave me. The Lord forgave me. And I forgave myself.

We need not look any further than our own back door. We stumble through, sometimes searching a lifetime for something that will bring us fulfillment, love, peace, balance, acceptance.

The good news is that God is never any further away than a whisper. Welcome home.

*F*ather, thank You for the experiences and blessings I've stumbled upon throughout my journey. Please keep the light on to always guide me right back home to You. *A*men.

"Do nothing at all unless you begin with prayer."

Ephraem the Syrian

"Hear my cry for help, my King, my God! To You I pray, O Lord; at dawn You will hear my cry; at dawn I will plead before You and wait." Psalms 5:3–4

There it is: shoved into the far depths of my closet, judging me every time I open the door. That little black dress—with dreams and ambitions of its own. Alas, a waistline suffering from one too many indulgences has sentenced it to a life of darkness far from the light of day or an evening out on the town.

Much like my real life, my spiritual life feels like a yo-yo diet at times. Sometimes I'm on fire; I watch what I eat, I workout.

Sometimes my devotion to prayer and grace is on fire, too. I find inspiration in unexpected places; I hear God's call in everyday ways.

And then there's times when I just get out a spoon and eat frosting from the container! (True story!)

A strong faith life demands dedication, practice and sacrifice.

Let Jesus be your personal trainer. Your faith is your little black dress; it's one size fits all AND you look amazing in it!

Dear Lord, thank You for loving me as I am and for loving me into being even more like You. I love You, Lord. Amen.

"When we are linked by the power of prayer, we, as it were, hold each other's hand as we walk side by side along a slippery path; and thus by the bounteous disposition of charity, it comes about that the harder each one leans on the other, the more firmly we are riveted together in brotherly love."

St. Pope Gregory the Great

"Good indeed is the Lord, whose love endures forever, whose faithfulness lasts through every age." Psalms 100:5

Lonely. Usually when you think of this word it's synonymous with being alone, without anyone around.

Why then, in a crowded room or a crowded house can you feel alone and lonely?

Words can be hurtful and isolating. So can a gesture or a look. Sometimes it's a feeling, a sense, that can put us into that state of loneliness. Most times it's those who are closest to us that can make us feel the loneliest.

When you cry yourself to sleep at night, who hears you? When you live within your own thoughts, who comforts you and eases your restless heart? When you have that pain that seems like it's in your stomach but it's really your own heart breaking, who holds you?

It is precisely these times when we need to stay within God's grace. Our best life is just on the other side. In the darkness of loneliness there is only His light. He is beautiful. God wants us to call on *Him* to fill our voids of loneliness. *He* loves us. Isn't that what really matters?

When we feel we can't rely on anyone else, there's always God. He's always there. He's waiting to take our hand. We only need to reach for Him. Reach for Him in your darkness.

Dear Lord, please continue to be a beacon of light and love. Help me to never lose sight of You. When I'm in my place of darkness, I pray, Lord, that You reach for me when I don't know how to reach for You. Thank You for always being here for me.
Amen.

"The cross is the gift God makes to His friends." St. John Vianney

"Jesus Christ is the same yesterday, today, and forever."
Hebrews 13:8

There are certainly things I'd love to redo if I could go back, like that first kiss with my then boyfriend and now husband. Or sneaking back into the house WITHOUT getting caught! I'd

go back to the moment my first child was born, and then the second, third and fourth, too.

I'd go back to the Thanksgiving three weeks before my dad died. I'd stare into his beautiful blue eyes again. I'd tell him how much I deeply love him and appreciate everything he ever did for me. I'd thank him for loving me unconditionally. I'd tell him how I think about him everyday — still, after five years. I'd tell him that I compare every man to him. I'd tell him how much I miss it when he'd answer the phone and I'd say, "Hi, it's me!" And he'd say back, "Hi, me!" God, do I miss him.

And then there is something to be said for unanswered prayers.

I don't want to go back to a life when I didn't know Jesus. Life was hard and empty at times.

The thing that I didn't realize until not too long ago is that God was there.

People we love will come into our lives and return to their heavenly home because we are all only on loan. While sometimes it's too late to say what's in our hearts to those loved ones, it's never too late to call on the Lord. He's always been here. And He'll always be here.

*D*ear Lord, thank You for the people You've put in our lives to keep us company on this journey.   *A*men.

"Love . . . the Apostle Paul declares to be greater than the other two graces, that is, than faith and hope . . . For when there is a question as to whether a man is good, we don't ask what he believes, or what he hopes, but what he loves."

St. Augustine of Hippo

"And the King will say to them in reply, 'Amen, I say to you, whatever you did for one of these least brothers of mine, you did for me.'" Matthew 25:40

𝒮now pants? Check. Mittens? Check. Hat? Check. Coat? Check. Sleds? Check, check!

I have a memory like a steel trap, which is sometimes a blessing and a curse. Today I am loving this memory, however painful it might be. Don't let me scare you. Read on.

I grew up in rural Wisconsin. You know, where it's snow and below zero for 9 months out of the year? Well, almost.

As a kid I loved to go sledding. Town kids came out of the woodwork on a snow day and my brother and I would greet the day and the rest of the kids at Mr. Wolfe's hill. He had a hill that seemed to be at just about a 90-degree angle. No kidding! We'd stand at the top of that hill, looking death in the face. And then hold on for dear life. The thing about this hill was that it ended abruptly with another hill ascending up to the street. So it was safe. As safe as a huge, steep hill could be!

On this particular day, as usual, my younger brother and I were at the hill. He had his steel runner, Radio Flyer sled and I held the bobsled-type plastic one. He went first. It was a successful slip but not as smooth as my plastic ride. He begged me to wait at the top of the hill for him so that he could use the sled next. As any good, big sister, I encouraged him to hurry and get his butt up there or I was leaving him! Well, the kid got half way up that hill and, again, as any good big sister would do . . . I went without him! Picture me sitting in my sled, holding on with a death grip, head down, laughing—that sweet laugh of evil.

The wind in my face, I was soon to approach my brother at mid-hill. He picked up that Radio Flyer sled and whacked me in the face as I flew by him! OUCH, to say the least. I lay on the ground, bloody, screaming, and holding my dangling tooth. Instantly, and I mean instantly, my brother starts crying like a baby. "I'm sorry. I'm sorry," and here it comes, "Don't tell mom!" So I'm lying there bleeding, thankful my head isn't laying next to me on the ground, and he's worried about me telling on him. "Please, Chris, don't tell mom!"

Instead of beating him to a pulp, we packed it up and walked home. I told him that I wouldn't tell. Of course, I didn't have to. My mom saw us coming from the kitchen window.

18

I know cutting my brother some slack and not telling on him won't make me a martyr, but it reminded me that even at that age I felt compassion for someone else and wanted to make him feel better, if only for that moment. I also may have been thinking that my parents would take care of him more than I ever could! (Again, the evil laugh!)

You know that when a child hurts, so does her mother and father. Just as we hurt, our Father hurts. He also takes delight in the good that we do in His name. What you do to and for others, you do for Him. Good or bad. For He is within all of us. Give glory to God today. Practice seeing Jesus in the people you come across today. Share your joy and your life. You will be giving so much more than you know. And God will smile.

*D*earest Lord, thank You for this day You have made. We give You glory and we praise You.   *A*men.

"Our sins are nothing but a grain of sand alongside the great mountain of the mercy of God."   St. John Vianney

"And over all these put on love, that is, the bond of perfection."
Colossians 3:14

*L*ove by definition: a strong positive emotion of regard and affection.

Love is one of the greatest commandments we've been given. Jesus tells us to love one another as He loves us. He even tells us to love our enemies.

I believe in love at first sight. When I met my children for the first time I was madly, insatiably in love with them. I love chocolate. I love pasta. I love the smell of magnolias in a warm summer breeze. I love the way my husband holds my hand when we go to sleep at night.

At times love is something we have to practice. We have to make a choice to love someone. Especially those who are cruel and who hurt us.

Loving the people who love us is easy. It's loving those who hurt us in all imaginable ways that's difficult and also where we find the most reward. It's how we learn who we are. We discover the depths of our own compassion. I've prayed for those who have wronged me. I have felt great peace with releasing the emotional hold that these people had over me. When I can say that I love them because they are children of God, as I am, I feel resolved. I'm able to move on. I'm not saying it's easy. But it's something we must do if we are to honor God and His commandments. At the end of the day if we can say to ourselves and the Lord that we've honored Him by loving our neighbors as ourselves, with a pure heart, we will be seated by Him in paradise.

A great friend wrote to me tonight and reminded me that there is beauty on the other side, usually beauty you never even knew was there.

*D*ear Lord, with Your love guiding me I will love unconditionally. I will forgive those who hurt me. I will be a light for all to see. Your love is everlasting. Your love is beauty. *A*men.

"Christ made love the stairway that would enable all Christians to climb to heaven. Hold fast to it, therefore, in all sincerity, give one another practical proof of it, and by your progress, make your ascent together."
Fulgence of Ruspe

"For God is the one who, for His good purpose, works in you both to desire and to work." Philippians 2:13

*A*re you a "go-to" person? Do you have a hard time saying, "No," or are you too busy and find it hard to say, "Yes"?

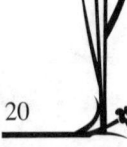

I've been thinking a lot lately about the sacrifice Jesus made for us. He knew that His purpose in His human life was to be the Son of God. He knew He was born a man to teach us God's law. He also knew that He would die for our salvation. His entire earthly life was dedicated to leaving a legacy: a legacy of everlasting life. And what did He ask in return? Only to be believed in and to be known as Christ our Savior. I'm speechless in gratitude and feel completely unworthy of Christ's gift at times.

Reflecting on the times I've been asked to help someone, I wonder how many times I've asked myself, "What's in it for me?" I've wondered if they would do the same for me if I needed help. How selfish!

Can you imagine if Jesus would have asked himself that? What if our salvation hinged on the answers to these questions?

Being someone else's salvation is a blessing and a gift. And by salvation I mean perhaps you've been asked to make a meal for a family during a difficult time, watch a child, give a ride, change a flat—or just be a shoulder to cry on, an ear to listen, and a friend to pray with.

My point is that it's not always convenient to help others. We all get busy. The next time you are called upon, I implore you to say, "Yes!" Despite your own busy, chaotic life, say, "Yes" and then pray. I promise you that He will make clear your way. The Spirit will give us the strength we need to be His faithful servants. We need only to believe in Him more than ourselves.

The road to your salvation is paved with the gifts you give others. Give and you will receive.

*L*ord Jesus, I can't express in words my gratitude for the life You gave for my eternal life in heaven. I want to be a vessel for Your Holy Spirit. Use me to do your works. Give me the strength and the courage to be a witness to Your truth.

*A*men.

"I began to understand that the love of the Sacred Heart without a spirit of sacrifice is but empty illusion." St. Maria Droste zu Vischering

"Jesus answered, "Will you lay down your life for me? Amen, amen, I say to you, the cock will not crow before you deny me three times." John 13:38

"Red Rover, Red Rover, send (anyone but Christine) right over!" Ever been there? Or remember playing kickball at recess? Were you ever picked last? I was. I'm not even sure why. I was a fast runner; I still am. Maybe I was too quiet and didn't sell my kick as well as I could have.

Instead of feeling elated at finally being picked, although I will admit I was relieved not to be standing alone any more, I was actually more of a leftover, a grumble. The last one to be called.

I wonder if that's how the Lord feels when we don't go to Him first. Does He feel like an afterthought? A last ditch effort. When there's no other choice, do we finally turn to Him with a grumble?

How is your witness? Do you give the Lord credit where credit is due? Do you wear your faith on your sleeve? Do you give thanks to the Lord for your blessings and repent for your sins?

If we can't say, "Yes," to these questions, we are no better than Peter. In John 13:38 Jesus is predicting the denial of Peter. He knew that Peter would emphatically deny knowing Him.

Let us not pick Jesus last. Thank Him for all that you are and all that you have.

Make God the captain of your team. He will lead you to victory every time!

Lord, may I never deny You again. I have fallen. I am a sinner and I come to You, Lord, for forgiveness. Thank You for being on my side always. Amen.

"Know, tyrant, that you cannot pluck my faith from my heart! Jesus Christ is my all-in-all, He is my treasure, my life, my bliss,

my capitol, my temple, my altar, and nothing can separate me from Him!"

St. Macra, as she was placed on the rack to be tortured for her faith.

"You are my refuge and my shield; in Your Word I hope."

Psalms 119:114

I woke up early this morning. Not for any particular reason. One minute I was sound asleep and the next my eyes just popped open.

"Thank you Lord for a good night's rest."

I lay there for a moment blinking, trying to focus my eyes. As I stretched, I could hear my tired muscles screaming from the previous day's run. I stared at the ceiling for a bit listening to the deep, rhythmic breathing of my sleeping husband. I thank God for him. Just having him near me makes me feel safe. Then I hear a lighter breathing, still rhythmic and deep. I peaked over the edge of my bed to find one of my children snuggled into a ball on the floor with only his little Spider Man blankie. How sweet, I think to myself. He must not have needed me, but only wanted me near enough to feel his own safety and security. And so I am thankful for him, too.

These mornings I cherish. The enchanting aroma of Taster's Choice fills my senses. Right on time.

Moving the covers ever so slowly, I reached for my robe and stretched as far as my legs could in order to clear the child lying beneath me. Tip-toeing my way out of the room, I am as quiet as a mouse, careful not to wake a soul.

This is my time: the time of day when the sun is barely over the hill, the dew still kissing the grass. I reach for my coffee and inhale its dark roast. Then I see it.

My bible is exactly where I left it the morning before. It calls to me with great enthusiasm. I love the feel of my great book. It's a soft leather with pages of tissue . The cover no longer lies flat; its corners are curled up and stand at attention, just waiting for me to explore its pages.

It's these mornings when all I can hear is the breathing of my sleeping family and my snoring dog that I find my sweet retreat into the Word of God. He always has a special message just for me. He has a special message just for you, too.

When we make time for the Word of God—whether it's five minutes or longer, morning or night, we are inviting Him into our lives. Sometimes He's just close enough to us to let us know we are safe and we are loved. He's the one lying next to us. He's sitting in the passenger seat during car pool. He holds our hand when we are unsteady and carries us when we feel we can't go on.

Be with the Lord today and feel His sweet embrace.

Heavenly Father, how I love Your Word. Speak to me so that I may listen. I feel so safe knowing that You are by my side. Please continue to guide me in Your way. Amen.

"Faith furnishes prayer with wings, without which it cannot soar to heaven."
St. John Climacus

"She has done what she could . . ." Mark 14:8

I felt so absolved when I first came upon this scripture. There are days, most of them, in fact, that I feel inadequate, lazy, not good enough. I wonder if I was a kind and caring mother today. Was I a warm and giving wife? Was I the kind of friend that others would love to have? Did I live within grace today?

I can get anxious and overwhelmed with my messy house. I currently have my very own Mount Everest of clean laundry on my bedroom floor. The dinner dishes did not get done tonight. The kids did not take a tubby. And I probably didn't give my husband the warmth he needs, either.

But, you know what? I spent individual time with each of my kids. I prepared Easter baskets to take to Grandma's. I tucked

everyone in with a smile, a hug, and a prayer. I even snuggled for a bit. I also spent time with God and His Word today.

"She has done what she could."

There are so many teachings from the bible that really speak to me, and this is one of them. It's become my mantra. I actually find myself chanting when I can do nothing more.

This particular scripture is taken from the time Jesus was anointed at Bethany. He and his disciples gathered for dinner just two days before the Passover. While Jesus was reclining at the table, a woman broke open a jar of very expensive perfume and, pouring it over Jesus' head, she blessed Him.

You see, she wanted to honor Jesus and, being very humble and not having anything else quite as beautiful and rich, she did what she could. It was all she could do to show her reverence, love, and respect. While the others who gathered in the room criticized her, Jesus praised her. He said, "She has done a beautiful thing."

"She has done what she could."

I think we can be incredibly hard on ourselves. Did you try today? Did you do what you could? Not what someone else expects. Did you do what you could . . . today?

The Truth is: God doesn't expect us to be perfect. He expects us to *try* to be. "Be perfect as your Father in heaven is perfect." Matthew 5:48. He knows we're not. We're human. Do what you can. You are not insignificant and neither is anything that you do when you live by the grace of God.

*L*ord, thank You for loving me as I am. I understand that I will totally miss the mark sometimes, but thank You for showing me the way back through Your Word. I will do what I can to please You. *A*men.

"Christ has made my soul beautiful with the jewels of grace and virtue. I belong to Him whom the angels serve." St. Agnes

"For I know well the plans I have in mind for you, says the Lord, plans for your welfare, not for woe! Plans to give you a future full of hope." Jeremiah 29:11

$\mathcal{I}$ am thankful that God has a plan for me. Most of the time I don't know which way I'm going. I feel like I'm having an early midlife crisis most days.

As far back as I can remember I only ever wanted to be a mom. I don't think I ever thought of having a "fall-back" job. Now in my 30s, I've had a great career as a stay-at-home mother of four. But as my oldest enters high school and my youngest is off to kindergarten, I'm having an identity crisis. Honestly, I don't think I thought much about this until I was asked recently what my plans were going to be for myself next year. As if my job of mothering was over.

And then I realized I didn't have a single clue what I was going to do. I don't really have any dreams of my own, not career wise anyway. The hobbies and interests I have are purely for enjoyment and offer no monetary compensation.

I've prayed often and have asked God, "Why don't I know what I want to be when I grow up? Where are my dreams?" These have become very emotional questions for me.

My answers were revealed in His Word. God knew me before I was born. He knows the plans He has for me. He came to me in a whisper. I heard in His breath that I need to be patient and that when my dreams are to be realized they will be revealed. I am exactly where I am supposed to be right now.

Are you in a dream rut? Do you struggle with where you are and where you want to be? Ask of the Lord that your dreams be revealed to you in His time, not yours. Ask to be made ready to go after those dreams. Thank the Lord for His goodness and His preparations. We are all a work in progress and need to be made ready for the plans He has for us.

And so, while I am currently suffering from the moans and groans of one too many peeps and chocolate bunnies eaten, I can delight in the truth that I am living my dream today, and

tomorrow is yet to come. I will make ready His way with patience and grace; and gratitude, above all.

$\mathcal{L}$ord, thank You for making me a work in progress. I trust in Your Word and Your love. I accept my blessings and my crosses to make myself acceptable to receive Your gifts. Please fill me with Your Holy Spirit to keep me strong. Help me to see Your hand in my life; guiding me, helping me, and loving me. $\mathcal{A}$men.

"God did not tell us to follow Him because He needed our help, but because He knew that loving Him would make us whole."

St. Irenaeus of Lyons

"For in Him we live and move and have our being." Acts 17: 28

$\mathcal{T}$he front of my house, which the compass says is north, is a shady place for most of the day. When we moved here two years ago, I created a beautiful little garden just steps from my front door. I admire the love I've put into this garden each morning. Because direct sunlight is only for a few afternoon hours, I carefully chose flowers and plants that would best thrive in those conditions of shade and moisture. I fertilize these plants. I dead-head when necessary, weed and water. The time and attention I take in cultivating my garden is evident by the beautiful blooms that spring up from the earth. The buzzing of the humming birds is like a sweet song I enjoy in the morning hours, sipping my coffee from the front step.

Unlike my little Garden of Eden by the front door, there's a crook between the house and the garage that doesn't see much sunlight at all. Hiding in the shadows are flowering shrubs and bushes that require light. These are noticeably smaller than they should be, their branches nearly void of leaves. I've never even seen them bloom. They have not been cultivated. I don't water or weed them, prune or fertilize them. I haven't even bothered to move them to a spot where they will flourish and thrive . . . yet.

Our faith life can be examined in the same way. It's not going to happen on its own. It needs attention and patience. It takes practice and time. By feeding our faith with the Word of God and cultivating it with His love, we too can bloom in His light. We can weed out the things that take us away from God, such as sin.

It's never too late to transplant yourself into being one with Christ. Make your garden grow—the garden of your soul.

*M*aster, You are the gardener of my life. I am made strong in You. Through Your love I am made whole. Thank You, Lord.
*A*men.

"We shall steer safely through every storm, as long as our heart is right, our intention fervent, our courage steadfast, and our trust fixed in God." St. Francis de Sales

"In peace I shall both lie down and sleep, for You alone, Lord, make me secure." Psalms 4:9

*A*hhh . . . the sights, sounds, and smells of summer are all so delicious. It's hard to imagine anything better. One of my favorite activities in the summer is camping. Just recently, my best friend and I took up the sport: the two of us moms and a gaggle of children. Heaven!

When I close my eyes, I'm taken back to our campground last summer. The breeze is warm. In one deep breath all the familiar smells of summer wash in like a flood: campfire, morning dew on the outside of my tent, bacon cooking over an open flame. I feel the warmth of the evening fire as the cool of the night draws near.

Later, while gazing at the stars through the window of my tent, I am overtaken with wonder at how wide and deep this world really is. God is so good to have created so much beauty.

In the still of the night, all cozy in my sleeping bag, I hear the chirping of the crickets and the love songs bellowing from the tree frogs. Memories of catching fireflies in jars and roasting marshmallows play in my head as if it was just yesterday when I was a kid. Now I can delight in the same pleasures as a mom.

My eyes are heavy and my own breathing slows in rhythm like that of the occupants in my tent. I lie there in peace, feeling safe in the Lord's hands and thankful for every minute of that day.

How many days go by when we feel we haven't taken the time to notice the beautiful landscape the Lord has painted for us. He wants us to delight in His work.

How many days have gone by in our lives where we've made the wrong choices and had the wrong priorities? Have you gone to bed feeling that guilt? Have you lain in bed with a heavy heart about something you said or did? Take care. Tomorrow is another day. With God's love and guidance, we are brought to peace. When we are at one with ourselves and the Lord, we can lie down in the safety of His hands knowing that He is ever present, ever loving and everlasting.

Father, I pray that I am never too busy to take delight in Your wonders. Accept my humble gratitude and be always at my side. I pray to You for peace and that I may continue to grow closer to You in your ways, O Lord. *Amen*.

"Withdraw often into the depths of your being and there with living faith rest on the breast of God, like a child, in the sacred silence of faith and holy love." St. Paul of the Cross

"Let us approach with a sincere heart and in absolute trust with our hearts sprinkled clean from an evil conscience and our bodies washed in pure water. Let us hold unwaveringly to our confession that gives us hope, for He who made the promise is trustworthy." Hebrews 10:22–23

From new life springs eternal hope. But what if that new life is taken from us? As in the case of babies who never meet their mothers. Or the "cure" that provided hope for a new life is snuffed out by a recurrence. Life stopped short at any age seems unfair. We cry out as Jesus once did, "Father, why have you forsaken me?" In anger and pain we may curse the Lord for the sorrow we feel, but in our weakness we are made strong. It is through these times, as difficult as it is to understand, we grow closer to God. He knows our pain. He feels our sorrow. We are His precious children.

I have held the hand of a grieving friend. I've been the shoulder to cry on. I've been the voice on the other end of the phone. The questions of why and how could this happen are repeated like a broken record. The answers to these questions which bring me comfort are the truths that God has a plan for all of us, and that our loved ones are now in the personal care of Our Lord, Jesus Christ. Their lives, no matter how short or long, were a gift to those of us who were touched by them. We will be forever changed having had them in our lives. Through their love, their presence, their being, they were our hope: hope for another day spent with them, hope for the future, hope and proof that God does exist.

Father, please look upon us with love. Thank You for the gifts You've given us. Continue to guide us in hope and faithfulness so that we may see Your glory. Hold us in Your loving arms.   Amen.

> *"Cast yourself into the arms of God and be very sure that if He wants anything of you, He will fit you for the work and give you strength."*
>
> St. Philip Neri

> *"I will give them a new heart and put a new spirit within them; I will remove the stony heart from their bodies, and replace it with a natural heart."* Ezekiel 11:19

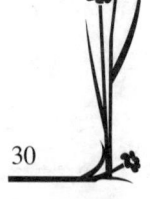

Admit one. That's what the ticket says. Come along with me now on the biggest roller coaster ever built with human hands.

Remain seated at all times. Arms up as the lap bar comes down.

Gulp. That's the sound your throat makes when it swallows your heart, forcing it back to its usual location.

Here we go! The car yanks forward, attempting to give you whiplash before you even leave the corral.

Thump . . . Thump . . . Thump . . . thump, thump, thump goes your heart.

Click . . . Click . . . Click . . . click, click, click goes the roller-coaster car up the first hill. The two in perfect time with each other. You're smiling and if you're like me, you may also want to cry or throw up!

It's a guarantee that this roller coaster is unlike any you've been on before, constructed with steep hills, plunging valleys, corkscrews, twists, and turns. Then at last, you're safely back in the corral. You step out of the car of terror with shaking legs and windblown hair, nearly out of breath and your heart racing faster than if you were on the treadmill. Amazed that you are still alive, you have the crazy desire to do it all again!

With all of life's hills, peaks, twists, and turns, we know that we have to go through the bad stuff, even scary stuff, to get to the good stuff. And we'd do it all over again to experience the thrill.

While we're on the mountaintop of our lives, when life is so good and going our way, we can and should thank the Lord for the blessings He's given us. We can trust that when we're slipping into the valley of tragedy, sadness, or anger, we can rely on God and His Church to be our lap bar— holding us tight, never letting go. He's with us until we're safe in the corral and in the peace and joy of our mountaintop once again.

Today accept God as a loving God. Moment by moment let Him into your heart. The Lord is our Savior. We shall not want for more.

Father, I love the way You love me. You shelter me from harm. You're never so far that I don't feel Your touch. Breathe a new life into me. *Amen.*

"God did not tell us to follow Him because He needed our help, but because He knew that loving Him would make us whole."

St. Irenaeus of Lyons

"Your love is before my eyes; I walk guided by Your faithfulness."
Psalms 26:3

*G*rowing up in a small town in Wisconsin, I was blessed to live at the foot of a beautiful bluff. Outfitted in long pants and sneakers, I loved to explore the hill. My goal, always, was to reach the top. Each journey held new surprises. It seemed as though I never took the same way twice. One foot in front of the other, twigs snapped beneath each step. The intoxicating aroma of pine and dried leaves swelled in the breeze. The only audible sounds were that of my breathing and the rustling of leaves.

Freeing myself from "pricker" bushes, avoiding poison ivy and digging my heals into the brush proved to be only part of my challenges. I realize now that the adventures on that hill were not only about exploration but also of escape. On that hill I could be independent. I could be brave. I could be myself. I was free from the anxiety, fear, and pain that plagued me. My journey was one of healing.

Once reaching the top of the bluff I would stand near a large rock and looking out over the tree tops I could see the river on the horizon. From that vantage spot, everything else was small: Everything but me. I was on the top of the world. On the top of that bluff I was more.

I have found myself climbing that bluff many times. Through relocations, infertility, death and births, and anxiety and depression, I have taken refuge in the Lord. Through Him I am made strong. I am brave.

Like my internal compass, which always helped me find my way home, safe, as a kid, the Lord is my north, and He brings me home.

We can feel safe and found in the Lord. He knows us, and through His Word He provides a loving path to Him.

*D*earest Heavenly Father, we come to You, Lord, lost and in need of Your love. Please guide our journey in Your loving grace. Be ever at our side. Be that sweet aroma on the breeze calling us home. *A*men.

"You must refuse nothing you recognize to be His will."

St. Jane Frances de Chantal

"He set me free in the open; He rescued me because He loves me." Psalms 18:20

"*C*atch me mommy. I'm going to fall backward." This cute and innocent request turned into an interesting game. I played along. I stood with my feet hip length apart, arms open, ready to catch Drew as he fell backward.

The first time he fell, I could feel his resistance. I told him, "Trust me. I'm here. I won't let you fall." With each descent into my arms, I felt him giving up control and letting go. What a powerful moment it was when he trusted me completely and fell into my arms. He didn't hold back. He just fell. And I caught him.

I wonder how many people I actually trust that much, enough to lay my life before them; not fearing judgment, resentment . . . or worse yet, rejection.

We all bear a cross. Sometimes our cross is obvious, everyone can see it, and at times we suffer in the dark, behind the smiles. A lifetime of hurdles, disappointment, and sin inhibit us from

reaching our full potential as Christians. There's always one place to go where you can lay down your life and be made whole again. When you "let go, and let God" you can begin to live. The Word teaches us to have the faith of a child. So when your Heavenly Father sings to you, "Trust me, I'm here. I won't let you fall," leave it all behind and fall. Fall in love with the Lord.

Father, I lay the pieces of my life before You. I pray You make a fresh start within my soul. Make me worthy of Your sacrifice that I may live to serve You. In Your Name, Amen.

"We shall steer safely through every storm, as long as our heart is right, our intention fervent, our courage steadfast, and our trust fixed in God."
St. Francis de Sales

"Be eager to present yourself as acceptable to God, a workman who causes no disgrace, imparting the word of truth without deviation." 2 Timothy 2:15

It may be too early in the season to be sipping my coffee barefoot out on my front step, but just try and stop me. I love the idea of going to bed at night if only for the thought of doing exactly this in the morning. It's the quiet time between coffee, God, and me; before it gets too noisy in my head . . . and my home.

Spears of lily of the valley fight their way through the fresh mulch. They strain and stretch upward, soaking in the warmth of the springtime sun. Peering down, between my irises and daisies, are small imprints. A closer examination reveals the foot print, or rather, the hoof print, of the deer who wished to graze on my baby foliage the night before. Fortunately I have some awesome spray that keeps them from enjoying the midnight buffet. But none the less, their imprint is there, a gentle reminder for me to take measures to protect my garden. It's the message that the deer leave behind that causes me to reflect.

I wonder about the imprint on others I'm leaving. Are people happy to see me coming or even happier to see me leave? Is my legacy going to be that of a woman who showed love for her neighbors and for God? Or do I appear to be lukewarm all of the time. Do I only wear my "Christian hat" on Sundays? Will I be remembered for my kindness and willing heart, or will I be the recipient of the "Could Have Tried Harder Award"?

More importantly, have I done my best for God? Would my best make Him proud? Through His Word we've learned that our best life can be discovered when all things are done for Christ. In everything we do and say, we alone have the ability to leave behind something wonderful. We can show our love and commitment to Christ in what and how we speak to others. Our actions define the life we live; may it be that of grace. When you do your best work He will be revealed.

Father, thank You for accepting my best and, through You, making it better. *Amen*..

"He who does not abide in his littleness loses his greatness."

St. Francis de Sales

"Love is patient, love is kind. It is not jealous, love is not pompous, it is not inflated, it is not rude, it does not seek its own interests, it is not quick-tempered, it does not brood over injury, it does not rejoice over wrongdoing but rejoices with the truth. It bears all things, believes all things, hopes all things, endures all things." 1 Corinthians 13:4–7

"Fire in the hole!" . . . "Clear!" And on this went for quite some time. My four-year-old sidekick and I were planting flowers, of course. I would dig the hole, hence the fire, and Drew would drop in the flower . . . clear! Life was good under the shady tree until my digging looked like a lot more fun than throwing a dumb old flower in the hole. And so, taking a

deep breath, I handed over my tiny shovel. What's that thing called again?

I looked at my watch. I looked at the sun moving across the sky. I tapped my fingers. I took very long blinks. All while one single hole was being dug. Boy, was I practicing patience. Tiny little hands have a hard time digging holes, I found out. It's not as easy as it looks, apparently. He needed to dig out just a little bit more dirt from our hole. In went the trowel. It dug deep into the earth, pushing aside worms, and, instead of scooping out the soil, that tiny little shovel, in those tiny little hands, flung dirt right in my face—open mouth and all. "Oh Lord, help me," I begged for more patience. I was already on my knees. Then a giggle. How funny to see mom eating dirt! Uh hummm.

As any good son would do, my sweet boy went into the house to get me something to quench my thirst. He reappeared in good time. He delivered, as promised, a tall glass of cold water. I took a drink. Yes, it was cold. And then an after-taste, of what I couldn't quite make out. So I held the glass like a fine, vintage wine. I swirled. I sniffed. Then I sipped again. It was a fragrant specimen. Flowery. Light. Almost recognizable. I asked Andrew, "Where did you get this water?" His answer, "The bath tub!" The water from the tubby he took the night before! And yes, I forgot to drain it. Lesson learned! Now do you believe God has a sense of humor!

We've all been helpless at one time or another. We've been weak. Riddled with sin. Plagued with addictions. The Lord still accepts us. He's patient with us, never angry. Our salvation is waiting for us. The bill's already been paid.

Love with your whole heart. Practice patience and love. You'll make your Father happy.

Dear God, help me to love others as You do. Work within me to be patient, especially when things aren't going my way. I pray that others can see Your light shining from within me. Thank You for Your love and for Your mercy. Amen.

"The spiritual virtue of a sacrament is like light: Although it passes among the impure, it is not polluted." St. Augustine of Hippo

"The boy grew up and the Lord blessed him." Judges 13:24

Tomatoes, peppers, and beans, Oh my! These are just a few of my favorite things! I've been flirting with the notion of adding a vegetable garden for a long time now, so this weekend I did exactly that.

I plotted out my own piece of choice property (in my yard) and got to work. Nothing to it, right? Wrong!

My shovel and I got to know each other well. By the end of day one I had a beautifully outlined 15 × 6 foot rectangle, which would be my garden. It's not huge, but it's all mine. Day two would serve to be a bit more challenging. My shovel went in and a chunk of grass came out; again and again and again. At one time, perhaps more than that, I'd look at how much I'd accomplished and then be overwhelmed at how much I had yet to do. I wondered if I could actually do this. It was proving to be a lot more work than I had imagined. I could see where I had started and how far I'd come, and I could envision the glory that awaited me once I finished. This kept me moving forward. It kept me digging. It was a test of my endurance.

I couldn't help but feel a deeper connection to this garden than I had anticipated. It was more than that sense of being one with the earth; more than the sower and reaper thing. It was a *spiritual* connection. It felt like a familiar metaphor of my spiritual life.

Today my hands and fingers are swollen. They ache from digging through the layers of soil and gravel. My legs hurt from kneeling and bending over. But, I did it! My vegetables have met their earthy home and the rain has just begun.

Once I was a shell of a person. A seed was planted within me and my faith began to grow. I know where I was and I know where I am. I can also see the glory that lies ahead of me. My faith journey has had many layers and continues to be uncovered. The journey hasn't always been beautiful; sometimes painful and ugly. But with hard work, commitment, and a greater vision, I am able to continue.

Heavenly Father, You are the Master Gardener. Thank You for planting your seed within me. Continue to nourish me so that I may continue to grow in Your love and be blessed.

Amen.

"There are, in truth, three states of the converted: the beginning, the middle, and the perfection. In the beginning they experience the charms of sweetness; in the middle the contests of temptation; and in the end the fullness of perfection." St. Pope Gregory the Great

---

"The Lord said to her in reply, "Martha, Martha, you are anxious and worried about many things. There is need of only one thing. Mary has chosen the better part and it will not be taken from her." Luke 10:41, 42

This is one of my favorite stories in the Bible. It tells of the sisters Mary and Martha. Jesus was invited into their home to gather, eat, and pray. Martha was a great hostess, tidying up, preparing meals, and making her home comfortable for her guests. Her sister, Mary, however, was quite intrigued by Jesus. She chose to sit at his feet and listen to his teachings rather than help Martha with preparations. The Word tells us that Mary has chosen what is best.

If you hang around me enough you will hear me remind myself to be a Mary, not a Martha. I enjoy helping my company feel as comfortable as possible when they come to visit. I try to serve their favorite snacks and drinks. Fresh flowers and pretty lotions by the bedside and a good book or magazine to curl up with at night are just a few of the things I enjoy doing for my guests.

I don't get crazy making sure the house is "white glove" clean. In fact, sometimes I intentionally don't vacuum just to tell myself that it's not what's important.

This passage helps remind me that it's the attention I give to my guests that's the better choice. They don't come to see my clean floors or dusted tables. They come to see me. I want to use my energy to enjoy our visit, not grumbling about all of the work I have to do to get ready.

This principle is also worth practicing with our family: the ones who live in our home. Things don't need to be perfect or always tidy. Grandkids or pets? The memories and the moments we create while we're together will last, not the tidiness.

Given that I have company coming the next two weekends, I have already begun to pray for perspective and peace. Certainly there are chores to be done in preparation, but not so many that I can't enjoy the anticipation.

The next time you're fussing before company remind yourself to be a Mary, not a Martha. When you can let it go and focus on what really matters, you'll be amazed at how freeing it really is. Give your worries and your anxiety to God. He will see you through. And make time for Him. When you make time for God, He will make time for you. Everything will come together.

Father, thank You for opening my eyes to what's truly important. I know that You will give me all the strength and energy I need to be here for others and to help them feel comfortable in my presence. Make my home a happy and loving place to be. *Amen.*

"We don't walk to God with the feet of our body, nor would wings, if we had them, carry us to Him; but we go to Him by the affections of our soul."
St. Augustine

"By wisdom is a house built, by understanding is it made firm; And by knowledge are its rooms filled with every precious and pleasing possession." Proverbs 24: 3–4

Drip, plop. Drip, drop. The rain has subsided for a short time, and what's left is the sound of water dripping from the gutters.

The sun that was so hot and high in the sky the day before is barely peeking out from the clouds today. And that's OK. After days of working in the yard, it's nice to take a rain break and reflect. I feel something new in me today. A calmness that's so refreshing. As if I've taken a deep breath and exhaled all the stuff that was weighing me down. Oddly, I don't feel anxious today or tired. Or sad or even mad. Today I am just me.

Cars break down. So do garage doors. Toilets overflow. Milk spills. The dog digs holes in the garden. Do you feel like your house is falling down around your ears sometimes? As if the paint might even blow off of the walls if you sneeze?

How do you react to unexpected inconveniences? Is there anger, worry, or disbelief? All of the above? How we choose to handle situations is what defines us. Maybe it's not about the world being broken. Maybe it's we who are broken. When there is something deep within our hearts and souls that needs repair, everything seems too big to handle. And we can choose to let it eat at us and take over.

The Lord is a magnificent handyman. His Word provides the necessary tools to make us right again. When we are one with God we can say, "Bring it on! Bring on the rain! I can handle it!" No job is too big.

The next time you're feeling as though the walls of your house are closing in, try this breath prayer: Breathe in and say Jesus. Breathe out and say Jesus. Say it as many times as you need to. In: Jesus. Out: Jesus. You feel better already, don't you?

*D*ear God, please make the necessary repairs within the home of my spirit that I may give myself completely to You. Let me be a witness to Your love. *A*men.

"*Lose yourself wholly; and the more you lose, the more you will find.*"

St. Catherine of Siena

"O Most High, when I am afraid, in You I place my trust."
Psalms 56:4

Sometime in between the still of the night and the screeching of the owls I felt a tapping on my shoulder. I blinked to focus and stretched out my arms to feel who was standing in front of me. Then a whisper cut through the darkness, "I had a bad dream."

As I walked her back to her room I tried to imagine what could have been so scary. As my daughter explained her dream out loud, neither of us could see why it was so terrifying. We talked about it, putting her at ease. I snuggled her and she fell back to sleep. Then I crawled out of her room and slinked back into my own bed.

There have been times in my life that I've buried emotions, events in history, and of course sin. Mistrust and painful memories are like debris in the water that keep coming up. Eventually you have to face it. Either you deal with these things or you are controlled by them. Sometimes it may feel easier to just barely live than to utter the regret out loud. Well, having been there, saying it out loud and dealing with it isn't as bad as I thought. Kind of like saying your bad dreams out loud; in the light of day and in safe surroundings, the fear is lifted. You can do the same with your fear and the bondage that binds it to you.

Abandon your fears at the foot of the Lord. Make your offenses known. Profess your regret. Make a vow of contrition. Don't live in your fear. Be free!

I have also been fearful of things I can't control: people and situations. Perhaps there are moments in your history as a child or just yesterday, in fact, that brought you to your knees in fear. And to that I say, "Thy will be done." I will not allow fear to distract me from my real purpose in this life. And you shouldn't either.

Lord Jesus, I no longer live in fear because You live within me. Thank You for Your gentleness. I reach for You in the darkness. You place a lamp at my feet. Amen.

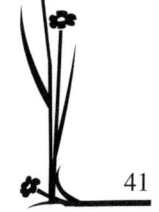

"Those whose hearts are pure are the temples of the Holy Spirit."
St. Lucy

"A faithful friend is a sturdy shelter. He who finds one finds a treasure." Sirach 6:14

They say no two snowflakes are alike. I've never held and inspected any, but I believe it to be true. That's pretty incredible. No two people are alike, either. And our friendships can vary as well.

Growing up, my best friend Shannon and I had a lot of fun making up dances to songs we taped from the radio, staying up late and talking about boys, and dreaming together about what we wanted to be when we grew up. I think we even vowed to live right next door to each other, too.

We don't live anywhere near one another now but we have rekindled our friendship. That's a testimony to a true treasure. Time and life went on, but our reunion felt the same as it did when I last saw her 20 years ago. What a blessing and a gift.

As an adult, I've made some friends and I've lost some, too. The greatest riches I have are the friends with whom I am able to share everything . I can be myself. They love me fat or skinny, cranky or happy. Like the snowflakes, my relationships with each of them are different, too.

I have the sweetest, most loving camping friend ever. We can put together a campsite like nobody's business. We can sit at the kitchen table and drink coffee in our jammies until noon, too!

Another inspires me to be the physically and spiritually best I can be. I have shared my journey with her. My love for God and life have expanded throughout our friendship.

And yet I have other friends I've never even met. We are pen pals who share a common goal of sometimes just getting through the day. We share our thoughts, ideas, concerns, and our love for life and our families who inspire us.

There's also my husband whom I love and adore beyond words. He's been with me through it all.

These are all my personal snowflakes, different and unique in their relationship to me.

It is only through my loving relationship with Christ that I've been allowed these treasures. Through Him I've been blessed to receive them. When we open ourselves and accept Christ's love, we are able to give and accept love to and from others.

Reflect on your treasures today. Give thanks to the Lord for those He's given to you.

Dearest Heavenly Father, You are the ultimate matchmaker. Thank You for loving me and giving me friends who love me and accept me. Help me to be a friend others would like to have. Your love is my deepest treasure. *Amen.*

"You, who have the kingdom of heaven, are not a poor little woman, but a queen."
St. Jordan of Saxony

"All flesh is like grass, and all its glory like the flower of the field; the grass withers and the flower wilts; but the Word of the Lord remains forever." 1 Peter 1:24–25

Judging from the position of the sun against the teal sky I'd say it's about three o'clock. But then again I'm on vacation, so who really cares what time it is!

The air is thick today, leaving my skin salty to taste and sticky to touch. Walking the shore line of the beach, with the surf licking the bottoms of my cuffs, seaweed rushes over my feet. Sand tickles my toes as the waves wash past me. As they retreat, the very foundation I'm standing on almost feels as though it is leaving, too. What's left behind are beautiful shells, different in size, color, and texture; shells worn down from being tossed back and forth with the tide.

Up ahead in the distance I can make out a castle. Little hands dug out a moat to protect it from intruders. Only a day before it had been a magnificent structure, but now it has fallen victim to the tide: Its walls dissolved and its once squared-off corners now rounded and slouching.

Further on still, driftwood, washed against the shore and showing its wear from the tide and current, now has become a popular resting place for the birds of the sea to feast on crabs that were washed up the night before.

Sitting now in the beach chair, my toes sifting through the sand, I can see nothing but ocean, a great expanse before me. I am reminded of how great Our Lord is. Like this ocean, His love is never ending. Not only has He created so much glory, but the thought that His dreams for us outnumber the granules of sand in this beach is breathtaking. And although life changes in the blink of an eye, or with the coming of the tide, His love never changes. It never disappears. The greatest things we experience in this life are nothing in comparison to our life in heaven. Live your best life. Give thanks to the Lord for being a witness to His beautiful handiwork.

Dearest Lord, thank You for saving a spot for me in Heaven. Please help me to take the time to enjoy Your beauty on this earth and in this life, as well as the people in my life who make it so special. I love You, Lord. *Amen.*

"There's nothing so great, my children, as the Eucharist. If you were to put all the good actions in the world against a Communion well made, it would be like a grain of dust against a mountain."
St. John Vianney

"My grace is sufficient for you, for my power is made perfect in weakness." 2 Corinthians 12:9

"Calgon, take me away!" Remember those commercials? On a Sunday not that long ago, I was standing in the eye of a cyclone—in my own home. The phone was ringing, kids were

running around crazy, bathrooms were dirty and the dog was tracking muck through the house.

A shroud of panic and anxiety overcame me. I could feel the blood rushing from my head and landing in my belly. For moments, it seemed I could hear nothing but my own heart beating and my own shallow breathing. Just then I sank into the pit of clean laundry waiting to be folded. By now it had been dug into several times and strewn across the floor. I lay there and cried; sobbed actually, and couldn't figure out why.

Sure my life with children gets very busy, between carpooling, volunteering and housework, but was this different than any other time? I poured my heart out to God. I wondered what was wrong with me. Why did it feel as though I was falling apart at the seams? Just when I would get myself under control, I would hear someone say my name, "Mom," that blessed name, and it would all begin to crumble again. Still, I had not reached out to God to help me, to save me from this moment.

It occurred to me, as life slammed into me, that I had been doing it on my own again. Somewhere between doing the morning dishes and running kids to gymnastics, I had decided that I didn't need to pray. I don't think this was a conscious decision, it just happened. I didn't make time for the Lord. And I don't believe that God punishes us or that He even tests us. His mercy and glory are greater than that. The truth is that we need to show the Lord our thanks everyday and in every way. When we get arrogant and think that we don't have the time or that we'll talk to Him when we need Him, our lives can become harried and empty.

Those times, when we hit our bottom and we are at our weakest, that is when the Lord is mighty. With His grace He picks us up; He carries us to the other side. It is through His grace that we are strong.

Someone once said, "If you're too busy to pray, you're too busy." If you make time for the Lord, He will make time for you. All things happen through Him.

*H*eavenly Father, thank You for Your grace. Please bless those who can't see the light at the end of their tunnel. May they come to know You through their weakness and feel Your loving hand. We love You and we praise You. *Amen.*

"However well you may run, however well you may wrestle, you still need Him who gives the crown." St. Gregory Nazianzen

"You need endurance to do the will of God and receive what He has promised." Hebrews 10:36

First the left, then the right. My shoes pound the pavement. And no, I'm not running from anyone! The motion is mechanical, my mind focused on the upcoming race. Dreaming of crossing the finish line, I am encouraged to keep going. Memories of a race I ran years ago inspire me that God made my body to move: Each part at one with the other. As I become more intent on getting through this training session, I unexpectedly take a turn off the beaten path. Although the rain begins to fall, I feel a calming sensation flood my being. I no longer feel labored with the pain in my knees, and my breathing takes on an almost relaxed rhythm. It is oddly quiet yet very serene now, with the drumming of my feet, my own breath, and the rain slapping the trees overhead.

Have you ever felt like giving up on believing in yourself, or worse, in God? When all around us there is so much doubt, it takes a lot of energy and love to continue to be a witness to Christ. Doesn't it seem easier to stay quiet and not be judged or hushed? I think of Jesus when I start to feel this way. He was ridiculed and treated harshly, yet He persevered. He wasn't always accepted, yet He kept on. His path had been the road not taken.

When in doubt, remember the love Our Father has for you: The salvation He has brought us is the medal at the finish line. Although we think we may not have the will to go on, our bodies were made to move, our hearts were made to speak and witness Christ's love. Never give up. It's worth the run.

*D*ear Lord, please fill my body with Your Holy Spirit. Make ready for me the way to be Your true disciple. Thank You for making me who I am. I accept Your will, O Lord, and I will sing Your praises! *A*men.

"The woman who stayed behind (at the tomb) to seek Christ was the only one who saw Him. For perseverance is essential to any good deed, as the voice of truth tells us: 'Whoever perseveres to the end will be saved' (Mt 10:22)." St. Pope Gregory the Great

---

"May all your enemies perish thus, O Lord! But your friends be as the sun rising in its might!" Judges 5:31

*G*ood morning beautiful world! Good morning to my garden! The forecast calls for a hot, sunny day. Since it hasn't rained in quite some time, relying on moist soil isn't an option today. Crank. Crank. I pull the hose from its box. The wet grass is cold on my toes as my feet slosh around through the yard. I drag the hose to meet the garden. Wake up flowers! My thumb is nearly covering the end of the hose, creating a spray to gently kiss the petals yet soaking the base of the plants. As usual, my hose doesn't quite reach the end of the garden and the force of water is not strong enough to be shot from across the yard to reach the tender, thirsty plants. So I retrieve my wide-mouth watering can. Lugging the heavy trough across the yard is a pain, yet, if I want to keep these flowers, it is worth it. The sun will be high in the sky soon, and without supplementing the rain with my watering, my garden will be scorched.

    I was thinking about how sometimes going to church to worship can seem like an out of the way thing to do sometimes, too. Isn't it just enough to be a good person? Isn't it enough to pray before I go to bed? The answer is clearly, "No," to all of these questions.

    We can do our best every day by trying to walk in the light of Christ, but without supplementing our goodness with the Word

of God and visiting His home to worship Him in the mass, we can find ourselves just going through the motions. We can become stale. It is the quintessential step in our faith life. Worship brings us closer to Christ. It makes us strong. We too need to go that extra mile to nourish our faith life. Let Christ sprinkle you with the goodness of His love. Walk for Him today.

Dearest Lord, I will walk for You. I will go the extra distance to taste and see Your love. Thank You for Your goodness. In all ways, You are my sun. You are my water. *Amen.*

"Sometimes, when I'm in such a state of spiritual dryness that I can't find a single thought in my mind that will bring me close to God, I say an Our Father and a Hail Mary very slowly indeed. How they take me out of myself then!" St. Therese of Liseux

---

"All good giving and every perfect gift is from above, coming down from the Father of lights, with Whom there is no alteration or shadow caused by change." James 1:17

"Mom, Do you know what I want to ask God someday? How did I get the best mom in the world?" From one of my cards on Mother's Day.

I had the very best Mother's Day EVER! Actually, the entire weekend was a gift from God. My twins celebrated their first sacrament of Holy Eucharist and my extended family trudged across state lines, enduring time, distance, sore butts, and a broken down car, all to be here with us. Not only were we celebrating the gift of Jesus through His body and blood, but we celebrated the gift of family. It was so precious to me.

Mass on Saturday was an emotional experience for me. I had the usual fatigue associated with being a good hostess, although I tried to practice being Mary, not Martha! But what was so sincerely moving to me was having my family sharing my space with me. The church was beautiful with flowers lining the window sills, the sunshine streaming in and lighting the altar. The organ chimed out, "Taste and See" while the violin kept its own time. Looking around at the members of my family sitting there with me, I felt enormously blessed and that many prayers had been answered that morning. In a moment, I realized exactly what is so important in my life: It is the love I have for God and for my family. Truly a gift from above.

I received many sweet gifts from my children and husband this Mother's Day, but the most beautiful gift was that of being with my family. God has heard my cries and answered. He continues to bring us closer through His love.

Dearest Father, I am a faithful servant. I love You, Lord, and I love the things You make possible through trusting and believing in You. Continue to work through me, Lord, in grace and love. *Amen.*

"Small vessels may hold great gifts."   St. Ephraem the Syrian

---

"Be glad in the Lord and rejoice, you just; exult, all you upright of heart." Psalms 32:11

How simply, yet masterfully said. Rejoice in the Lord. This verse in inscribed in the bubbly little fountain I have perched on my garden table. As I sit here this morning listening to the plip, plop, tinkle, tinkle of the water, I nestle in to sip my coffee. The rain the night before has left behind a crispness in the air. The light breeze has an intoxicating scent of the newly bloomed iris floating in its breath. Closing my eyes and taking in the sounds of the morning, I am thankful for yet another day to enjoy the glory of this beautiful landscape.

I am not the kind of gal who jumps out of bed in my tennis shoes and hits the ground running. I am more of the sort who slowly slips my toes followed by my heels into my slippers, stumbles to the kitchen, flicking on little lamps, and lighting

candles as I go, kind of gal. This is how I begin my day. And I like it.

As the house begins to yawn and stretch and come to life, I pray to our dear Lord to watch over us all and to continue to bless us with health, happiness, and love.

I pray today that the Lord enters the hearts of those who have little faith or for those who have been hurt and turned away from God. May they feel welcome to come back to the Father and receive His love. I pray that we are always able to rejoice in the Lord and see the good around us every day. The love of the Lord is in every person and He is in us. Open your hearts to Him today. He is ready and waiting for you.

*D*ear God, give us the faith of a child. Although we think we cannot see or touch You, help remind us that You are always here. We need only speak Your name. Thank You for Your tender mercy and the love of a Father only You can give.

*A*men.

"I do not lend. I give. Hasn't the good God been the first to give to me?"
St. John Vianney

"Jesus looked at them and said, "For human beings it is impossible, but not for God. All things are possible for God."
Mark 10:27

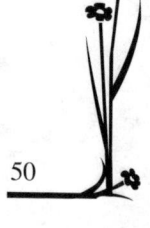

*H*appily dreaming about fishing and gardening and playing in the sun, I am jolted awake with the realization that today is the day I get to go play with my girlfriends! Wanting to lay in bed for just a minute longer is not going to happen. My mind is already racing and checking off the list. I do pause, however, to remember that I need to ask for help today. If I am going to accomplish everything I feel I need to, there is only one being who can make that happen. You guessed it: Our God Almighty. So to start my day, I ask our Heavenly Father to please be with me; be the wind beneath my feet this morning. Help me to be calm, organized, still loving and patient with my children and husband. And in all these things, thankful that I am loved and cared for by Jesus.

As I'm getting children ready for school and kissing the hubby good-bye, I glance at my watch, over and over. I'm amazed that time seems to be standing still. In a very short amount of time I have accomplished great things, even watered my precious gardens. Sitting here, writing this now, is proof that the Lord has filled me with His Spirit. Through Him I am here. And so, I am packed, kids are off, and I'm on my way. The sun is shining and so is the Son!

I pray for you all that, while you may be busy and overwhelmed with activities or just plain life, you take the time to reach out to Our Father. Ask for His assistance. He will be your wind!

*D*earest Lord, please bless all of my dear friends today and guide them in Your way. Help them to reach for You and to know You are there. Through You all things are possible. For safety, peace, and love. *A*men.

"God is not contained, but is Himself the place of everything."
St. Theophilus of Antioch

"Let your life be free from love of money but be content with what you have, for he has said, "I will never forsake you or abandon you." Thus we may say with confidence: "The Lord is my helper, and I will not be afraid. What can anyone do to me?" Hebrews 13:5–6

*M*y head nods. My eyes are blurry. Tummy rumbling. The wind in my face isn't enough to keep me awake during the long car ride home. Music blares from the radio, but even that sounds like a lullaby. I even start singing out loud and still that's not enough to help me focus on the road. So I resign myself to pulling over at a rest stop for a breather. It's so quiet here. The sun, about to set, is just twinkling between the leaves as they rustle softly in the trees overhead. There's an odd silence, odd because this stop is just off the interstate. And although I can see the road from my car, I can hear only the birds bidding the day farewell.

I make an effort to try and see Jesus in all people and every way when possible. I don't believe God tests us, but gives us opportunities to show our faith, love, and commitment to being a good Christian. When there is someone in need, someone hurt, a distressed animal perhaps, we have the opportunity to let Christ's love shine through us by being their savior.

Walking back to my car from the shelter in the rest stop, I was stopped abruptly by a woman blocking my path. Just behind her stood a burly man . I couldn't see his eyes; they were shielded by sunglasses with only the trees reflecting back at me. The woman was very thin and had almost a wild look in her eyes. She asked if I might be willing to help them out; they needed money for gas. She had a sketchy story as to why they had the troubles they were having. As I was listening to her, I was frozen still. I couldn't see Jesus in her eyes. I couldn't see Jesus in the way the man was standing behind her. I had the eerie realization that I was alone in this rest stop with just the two of them. I fumbled through my purse and revealed a five dollar bill, hoping that was enough to satisfy them. I nervously explained that it was all I had. Not taking my eyes off of them, I continued to walk to my car. My keys fumbled in my grip and clumsily opened the locked door. Driving off before buckling, I thanked the Lord for not abandoning me. I thanked Him for keeping me safe. I don't know for certain what these strangers' intentions were, but I was frightened. I pray that Jesus enters their heart and finds a better way for them.

And so, I will not stop letting my love for God shine through in all things that I do. I will smile at people. I will offer a helping hand when I can, for He has breathed His breath of life into me. As a called servant, I shall do His will. Perhaps, though, I won't stop at an unattended rest stop in the future!

*D*earest Lord, I love You for Your care. Thank You for being my guardian and my light. I praise You in all ways and pray that You continue to enter the hearts of those who are lost and hurt. Help them find their way to You, sweet Lord.

Amen.

"Take away all evil, and much good would go with it. God's care is to bring good out of the evils that happen, not to abolish them."
St. Thomas Aquinas

"Once more will he fill your mouth with laughter, and your lips with rejoicing." Job 8:21

The garden is particularly busy this morning. Too witt too witt too whoo. Tweeter tweeter tweet. I don't know the names of all of the birds I hear and see pecking through the dew soaked grass, but their greetings are welcome this morning. It's like a scene out of the Snow White film. Deer walking within feet of me, snacking on my bushes, and chipmunks scurrying across the walk, stopping long enough to see if I'm friend or foe and then back to work. Out of the corner of my eye I see the sliver of a spider's thread extending from the bird feeder to a branch. Busy, busy morning. My morning will not be so busy. I have burdened myself with the guilt of being a tired, cranky mother the night before. Were the kids really so wild? Did the day really fall apart? Was there anything so bad that actually happened to me to bring on the crankies like it did? Probably not. But I allowed little things to affect me. And when I'm disturbed, guess what? Everyone else feels it, too.

Before my walk I closed my eyes and looked up to heaven. I prayed for peace of mind and to still my heart. I prayed for patience, love, and understanding. I prayed for help. And I prayed for continued guidance. No matter how much I read, no matter how faithful I truly am to serving the Lord, I have bad days, too. Of course! I am human. But I am a Christian. It is my faith in God Our Father that allows me to go on yet another day and gives me the chance to start over. He gives me the chance to do it better today.

The sweet sounds of this morning remind me of a love song playing over and over again in my heart. My love song is to the Lord. In spite of and because of my sins, He gives me new life and I am able to accept it. I want to be real. God looks into my heart and sees me. He knows me. I dedicate this day to loving the Lord and glorifying Him in my work. May we all give up our selfish ways today. Put the Lord first, and in thanksgiving ask for His hand in leading you to eternal joy. Shout from the rooftops and proclaim Him as your Savior.

Father in Heaven, please hear my song! I love You for everything that You are! Thank You for seeing the real me and saving me from myself sometimes. Help me to glorify You in everything that I do. I pray that my loved ones and the friends I haven't even met can see Your love shining through me. I have learned that You are so good! *Amen.*

"Mother dear, lend me your heart. I look for it each day to pour my troubles into."
St. Gemma Galgani

"Before I formed you in the womb I knew you, before you were born I dedicated you, a prophet to the nations I appointed you."
Jeremiah 1:5

Today is my baby's birthday, although he fervently disagrees when I refer to him as my baby. I was told not to buy any baby toys this year! Only the cool big-boy stuff like swords and some claw thing. Before getting ready for school, he put on his daddy's cologne and wanted to gel his hair! They grow up fast. I told my "baby" that it was my birthday today, too. It was five years ago today that I gave birth to him and the day I fell in love. I anticipated his birth for nine months. Dreaming of who he'd be and who he'd look more like: my husband or me. Looking at our other three children, I already knew whom he'd take after. But I also dreamed of more than his appearance. I wondered about his personality: Would he be a serious person or more care free? Would he be clumsy or strive for perfection? Would he be athletic or more creative in an artistic sense? Would he share my love of the outdoors or his father's love for a good book? Or both?

Well, like my love and anticipation, our Lord anticipated my son's birth as well. Our Heavenly Father knows the answers to all of these questions and more. He knew us before we were formed. Before we were ever a thought in our mother's mind. He knows the dreams He has for us. I believe He takes great delight in watching us become whom He knows we will be. Like mothers and fathers in this life, He's there to guide us and to care for us. God fell in love with us before *we* were born, too.

Father, thank You for the life You've given us. It brings me so much happiness to know that You have a plan for me. I take comfort and great joy in knowing that You are pure love. You are my friend and my Father. Amen.

"Let no one tell you that this body of ours is a stranger to God."
St. Cyril of Jerusalem

"Whoever clings to me I will deliver; whoever knows my name I will set on high. All who call upon me I will answer; I will be with them in distress; I will deliver them and give them honor. With length of days I will satisfy them and show them my saving power." Psalms 92:14–16

Liquid fence. What an awesome concoction! One part nasty and two parts stinky. Whatever it takes to keep my garden safe. This all but impenetrable spray is what keeps my flowers and spirits alive. Diligently spraying it, creating a fortress that surrounds the tender blooms, I can rest easy at night knowing that they will all still be there in the morning. Except for when I forget. Yes, it happened. I became too busy to tend to my garden and watch over them. And while my head lay softly on my pillow, the deer ravaged my spring harvest.

Stepping out with my coffee in hand, I admired the fountain, bubbling with happiness at yet another day. The hummingbirds were cheerful, too. Then I spotted them: Plants eaten to a nub. Oh the carnage! There was no denying who or what had visited me the night before.

I am very much relieved that God is in charge of taking care of us. There's never a time that He forgets. He is always present. His love, His Church, is our shield, our liquid fence if you will. He is all love, pure joy, and beauty.

Temptation and sin are at our doorstep constantly, sometimes very obvious and other times disguised. The Lord will not forsake us. He will cover us in His tender care, if we ask Him. And in all things give thanks to Him for His saving grace. We can rest easy at night knowing that Our Shepherd is always on watch. He will be there in the morning, noon, and night.

*D*ear God, thank You for holding us, protecting us, and watching over us always. I love the home You've made for me; pure joy, pure beauty, and only love. Blessed be Your name.

*A*men.

"Whenever you seek truth, you seek God, whether or not you know it."

St. Edith Stein

"Like a shepherd He feeds His flock; in His arms He gathers the lambs, carrying them in His bosom, and leading the ewes with care." Isaiah 40:11

A guinea pig, a lizard, a fish, and a dog. Sounds like the beginning of a real knee-slapper. Actually, the joke is on me I think. These are the pets who occupy our home. You'd think it was enough, right? Not so much. At times it would appear that we are running a mini wildlife refuge compound right here in our home. In fact, most recently added to the role call is a raccoon.

Just as dusk approached, skeeters (that's what my kids call them) flogging our tender skin, we were rummaging through the yard looking for a turtle friend who narrowly escaped the lawn mower just moments before. Walking deeper into the yard, peering closer, I realized I was staring into two tiny bandit eyes. Curled up into a ball like a kitten, breathing deeply, lay a raccoon. He was not in a tree, however, but in a live trap that my neighbors had set. Can you even believe my luck? This raccoon was discovered by the youngest members of the PETA group, and as their leader they begged me to set him free. Now, I am smarter than that, but I was diligent: I called the neighbors and left a message about how we are on the clock and watching out for this guy. Then I chopped up apples and sprinkled them in his cage. He snarled and hissed and even growled at me. I didn't take much offense as I'd probably do the same.

I love this scripture found in Isaiah. How tender and loving Our Lord is. He gathers us in His arms: those who follow and especially those who are lost. He holds us close and gently. Never leading us astray, and with His Word He feeds us.

We, too, can be like the Good Shepherd with our friends, family, and especially young children. We can hold our loved ones close, teaching them the way to the Lord if they are lost; gently holding them near. We can show them the road map to Christ's love and tenderness through our words and actions.

*D*earest Shepherd, we are Your flock. We turn to You, O Lord, for Your gentleness and loving nature. We accept Your will and praise You, Lord, for Your goodness and mercy. *A*men.

"Seeing God means following Him wherever He might lead."
Gregory of Nyssa

"I give thanks to my God at every remembrance of you, praying always with joy in my every prayer for all of you."
Philippians 1:3–4

*H*i God. It's me, Christine. Are you there?

Silly question, really. My prayers at times start out real formal, almost as if I'm introducing myself for the first time. It takes practice in remembering that the Lord and I are close, long-time friends. Of course He's here. He also already knows what I'm going to say. It's an interesting truth: Our Lord is so mighty and knows us so well that He knows what we are feeling and what we're going to say before we even speak. He sees into our hearts.

Have you ever wished you had your best friend by your side all of the time? Not only in troubling situations but to witness the good stuff, too? Or to bounce an idea off of or to check yourself? Well, guess what? He is! He's been here the whole time. Remember that and start a conversation. It might go something like, "Nice day today. Thanks!" or "Why am I so tired today?" "I wonder if I'll be able to get my work done with so much to do." Anything really. He doesn't mind listening to you. Don't feel like you're talking to yourself, either. He's there. If you think it is a one-sided conversation, think again. If you listen closely, you can hear Him answering and even speaking to you. It may feel like intuition or a gut feeling. Your answers may be found in the completion of a task, an illness cured, an energy boost, or a smile from a stranger. All of these things and more are your proof that He exists and that He hears you.

God, Our Father, provided His friendship and guidance that can be found in His Word. Christ is "the Word made flesh" and, through His Church, the Holy Spirit guides us. But, the bible is also a resource to confirm our faith and the Church's teaching. Because God knows us so well, He knew that we would need a place to go to find the answers. When we don't know how to listen or it seems too hard, the Word and the Church are there for us. Turn to Him today in any way that you can. Strike up a conversation with an old friend. He's listening!

*D*ear God, I know You are there, standing always at my side. You love me. I thank You for Your Son, Jesus. I thank You for the blessings You lay at my feet. Help me to see Your glory and to hear You. I praise You and I love You forever and ever.
*A*men.

"Lord, You called to me and cried aloud, and You broke through my deafness. You flashed, and shone, and chased away my blindness. You breathed upon me fragrantly; I drew in my breath, and now I pant for You. I tasted and now I hunger and thirst for You. You touched me, and I burned to enjoy Your peace."
St. Augustine of Hippo

"There is an appointed time for everything, and a time for every affair under the heavens." Ecclesiastes 3:1

As I dust off the camping gear of tent, lawn chairs, lantern, and the fire poker, the memories of last years' adventures play in my head. Will our adventures be as exciting this year? Where will we go? How long will we be gone?

Sitting near the campfire after a long day of floating, running ragged and getting good and dirty sounds so refreshing to me, especially after such a busy year, full of school and sports and sacraments and camps. The list goes on and on. And although I'm happy the season is just beginning, I can't help but feel sadness, too. My oldest will enter high school and my youngest will be off to kindergarten. The other two shuffled in the mix. And somewhere within all of this my husband and I will try to find ourselves and where we fit into this world.

I am reminded by Ecclesiastes that we all have a season. In the midst of the chaos of everyday life, perhaps we all take turns entering our own season. It is important to take advantage of moments in this life that catch your breath and opportunities that provide portals to a better place and stage in our season—and patience enough to realize that it will be our turn.

Enjoy the blessings you've been given today. Take a moment to reflect on those around us who reflect God's love and grace. Spread your love to those who need it today. Give them the opportunity to see Christ; it may be their only opportunity for a while.

𝒟earest Lord, I pray to be an instrument of Your peace. Please fill me with Your grace. Allow me the patience to wait for my season, but to be supportive and loving to others while they are in theirs. Help me to see the love You bring to my life, and please continue to enrich the lives of those around us with the many blessings of Your mercy and grace.
Praise to You, Lord. 𝒜men.

"In a higher world it is otherwise; but here below, to live is to change, and to be perfect is to have changed often."

St. John Henry Cardinal Newman

"Therefore, our God, we give You thanks and we praise the majesty of Your name." 1 Chronicles 29:13

𝒞rrrreeeek. Mmmmph. Thud. The light goes on. And I squeeze in. No, it's not a crawl space or the attic. It's my closet. I have a space that is all mine and all messy. It's where I throw extra stuff, and when I can't find something, I know that it's probably in there. What a shame to use that closet like a junk drawer. "Someday," I say, "someday . . . ."

Back to my point: I was digging through the mound of "stuff" in there the other day, resembling a squirrel rummaging the leaves for a nut, and I came upon a journal. Its flowered cover, made of cloth, once was white but now is a faded gray. I hadn't seen this journal in years. I wasn't searching for it, but the mystery isn't about what's in my closet, but more of a miracle that I find anything at all! Opening its pages was like stepping back in time—a time of about 13 years ago. Within those pages were documented birthday celebrations with my older daughter, memories of holidays with family, disagreements and resolutions with my husband, job promotions, gardening . It was a time in my life when we didn't have much. We didn't have big jobs or a big house or a big family full of wonderful children. We didn't have much of a faith life, either.

I wondered, why now was I finding this journal? Why, after all these years of not seeing it, or choosing not to, perhaps, had it fallen back into my hands? As I finished reading the last entry, I realized why God had placed this in my hands. I needed to take a moment to reflect on where I was and where I am now. I needed to remember how God has blessed my life over the years and how even though I didn't know He was there, way back then, I could see His glory written all over those pages. What a gift this was to me.

Although some of those more simpler times have passed, other more important times have taken their place: the love for my husband has reached an indescribable depth, my faith has soared to unimaginable heights, and the love for my children and family is more than I can put into words. I would be lost without all of these blessings in my life.

Why not take some time today and remember the times that God was there for you. It's a trip down memory lane worth taking!

Dear God, thank You for being here for me. Thank You for counting me among Your blessings.   *A*men.

"My soul and his soul were but one soul in two bodies."

St. Augustine of Hippo

"Let us greet Him with a song of praise, joyfully sing out our psalms." Psalms 95:2

This morning started out just like the last couple of mornings; rainy and dreary. The one difference today is that the kids are out of school for the summer! As I was making a sack lunch for my husband to take to work, the breakfast orders came rolling in from the little people who like to rule my life. In addition to a short-order cook, maid, spiritual director and guide, my kids like to think of me as the entertainment committee as well.

So the questions of "what are we going to do today?" came rumbling in. All of them talking to me at once.

While pretending to listen (ha) I looked up and saw a rod of sunshine poke through the clouds and highlight the deck umbrella and the marigolds below. I broke out in song, "Praise the Lord for the sunshine! Praise the Lord for yet another day with my husband and children."

I have a towel in my kitchen that reads, "My other house is cleaner." That is a story for another day. Until then, the sun is still shining. The breakfast orders are still coming in. But I will choose happiness today. I will choose to love today. And I will choose to live today.

I pray that you are able to see the good that God brings to your life. Praise Him in song, whatever song comes to you. For the lips speak what the heart feels.

Father, praise to Your glorious name. I love You!   *A*men.

"Let your speech be brief and savory."   St. Ephraem the Syrian

---

"The Lord, your God, is in your midst, a mighty savior; He will rejoice over you with gladness, and renew you in His love, He will sing joyfully because of you." Zephaniah 3:17

*F*irst my big toe taps the surface, testing the temperature of the water. I snap it back out of reflex. That water is cold! How can these children swim in these frigid waters? Jumping in with both feet, fully submerging themselves, and then laughing about it? The warmth of the sun draws me to the water's edge. Perfectly content just dangling my legs doesn't last long, so I jump in with both feet. Nose plugged, I sink to the bottom. Sitting there for a moment, recovering from the shock of the temperature, I open my eyes and look around. How peaceful, I think. The sounds from above the water are only a dull echo below the surface. My arms, legs, and hair move in slow motion. Just for a moment, all of the things that lay heavy on my heart come to surface. And I make a choice to rid myself of those feelings.

Arising from the water, the worry and the hurt that I was carrying rested on my skin like the beads of water gathering there. As I dried off, I wiped those feelings away with them. I asked the Holy Spirit to guide my thoughts and actions in a caring way and fill the space within my heart with His joy and happiness, replacing the wounded feelings I had.

There are moments all around us put there by the Holy Spirit to calm us and bring us back to His heart. If we slow down enough and ask to see Him, He will show us He is there.

A song sung multiple times in my home this weekend and still ringing in my head today is not a song of praise, per say, but more of a reminder to me of where my true happiness and love lies: in the Lord above all and in my family. And so I leave you with a few lines from the most famous song in our house, and I give thanks to my husband for putting it there! "On top of spaghetti . . . all covered with cheese, I lost my poor meatball when somebody sneezed," and so on.

Dearest Lord, we come to You with praise and thanksgiving for the work that You do within our hearts to make us whole again. We thank You for Your Holy Spirit, Who works within us all to make us stronger and bring us closer to You. Thank You for the moments of pure joy when we are able to bring our hearts to You. Help us to never wander too far and help us remember Your song which leads us home. *Amen.*

"Let us imitate what we shall one day be." St. Cyprian of Carthage

---

"Then the Lord will guide you always and give you plenty even on the parched land. He will renew your strength, and you shall be like a watered garden, like a spring whose water never fails." Isaiah 58:11

Remember those days of summer when the rain pounds the rooftops and floods the gutters? And then the sun breaks through the clouds, shoving them aside as if to say, "That's enough!" Steam rises from the blacktop as the last of the storm is burnt off.

The flowers, previously drooping on each other in weak protest of the summer's heat, now stand upright and tall, thankful for the downpour.

I can relate well to this scene. I can go strong for so long and then fall victim to the "heat." It's when I cry out to the Lord for His guidance that He showers me with His love. I wonder why it is that although I know where to go for help and guidance that I continually try to do everything on my own. And just when I'm asking myself, "Why is this happening to me again?" or, "Why can't I do this?" it's an AH HA moment! I can be so blinded by what's in front of me that I can't see what's within me; what's been in me all along. It's Christ's love guiding me and loving me. If we only turn to Him in the heat of our day, He will pour down on us and save us.

When you start to ask yourself why, how, or what, have yourself an AH HA moment and thank the Lord for being in your life and ask Him to continue to bless you with His presence.

Father, thank You for Your rain of love and of hope that You pour upon my soul. I love You for Your goodness, Your kindness, and Your mercy.   Amen.

"Whoever possesses God is happy."   St. Augustine of Hippo

"Come to Me, all you who labor and are burdened, and I will give you rest. Take My yoke upon you and learn from Me, for I am meek and humble of heart; and you will find rest for yourselves. For My yoke is easy, and My burden light." Matthew 11:28–30

When I first read this scripture quite some time ago, I wasn't quite sure what it meant. I didn't know what a yoke was and couldn't quite "see" it. I've learned since that a yoke is a wooden bar used to pair oxen when plowing the fields. It allows them to work together as a team. They pull the load together and work in time, relying on each other's strength. Oxen almost always work in pairs.

I spoke to a dear friend today and she explained that she needed to "download" for a bit. She was apologetic in her introduction. But what are friends for, if not to be there to listen and to comfort? For today, my burden is light and I'm able to be here for her. I have been so amazingly blessed with deep and beautiful friendships in my life. There are times when I can give and times when I am able to receive. And sometimes we all "just get through the day" together.

Matthew 11:28–30 is such a sweet whisper in my heart. Although I was once confused by this passage, I now take great comfort in it. God wants to work as a partner in our lives to lighten our load. He is that dear friend on the other end of the phone. He wants us to come to Him with our worries and our cares. Sometimes we may feel we have nowhere to go or we don't have the words to explain how we are feeling. Understanding that God knows what's in our hearts and He knows our needs and He knows how best to help us can bring great peace and strength. We need not speak the words that are difficult to articulate. Go to Him today. Ask Him to hear what's in your heart. Ask Him to guide you in the way to your peace. Give yourself up to His Holy Spirit. Allow it to fill you and show you the way. God is with you and on your side. He is your rock when you feel you have nothing else.

Dearest Father in Heaven, we thank You for Your strength and Your light. Thank You for showing us the way to Your salvation. Thank You for being our friend and light in the darkness. Help us to be humble and merciful in our ways. Sometimes the day is long and we thank You for lightening our load. Amen.

"God passes through the thicket of the world, and wherever His glance falls He turns all things to beauty."   St. John of the Cross

---

"All the paths of the Lord are faithful love toward those who honor the covenant demands." Psalms 25:10

The tires of my ten speed burn the pavement with only the heat that a 12-year-old can create. Coasting downhill is fun. It's the easy part. But uphill, the climb is exhausting. Delivering newspapers as a kid, I rode that bike all over my small town. Homes were spread out, not at all close to one another. And I didn't just throw the paper in the driveway; I took it to the door and put it inside the screen or in the mailbox. Talk about service!

There was a road that I wasn't at all comfortable riding down, but there was a house at the end that I delivered to, so it was necessary. I recall there being a house that I would pass, and as I did so I would ride as fast as my legs could pedal. I don't know why, but it scared me. Well, wouldn't you know it, but I blew a tire on my ten speed and had to walk the route one day. As I trudged along that long, gravel road, I was approaching the house that had haunted me seven days a week. Staying on the left side, keeping a watchful eye on the front porch, a light breeze blew past me and the perfumed scent of peonies floated in its wake. Even then as a kid I appreciated the sweet smell in a summer's wind. I looked around to see where the aroma was coming from. Following the scent the way a hound follows his nose, I spotted them. The gorgeous blooms were planted right outside the front porch of the home I always tried to avoid. And in that moment I wasn't afraid anymore. This house, that fell abandoned and lay in disrepair, being nearly swallowed up and eaten whole by the grass and weeds around it, took on a beauty to me that day. I didn't see the ugly, the old or the scary. I saw beauty and what it once may have been.

Sin and tempest can take us to places we don't want to be. It can be easy to fall into temptation and participate in acts of unkindness and ugliness. These things take us further away from

God's truth and love. Through His Word we can be redirected onto the path of righteousness. Let others see your true beauty among the weeds and let them see the potential of who you can really be: One with Christ and love.

Dear God, thank You for Your everlasting kindness. Thank You for the beauty You represent. I love You. Amen.

"Christ has made my soul beautiful with the jewels of grace and virtue. I belong to Him whom the angels serve." St. Agnes

---

"The favors of the Lord are not exhausted, His mercies are not spent; they are renewed each morning, so great is His faithfulness." Lamentations 3:22–23

Skipping stones. I can't do it. I've tried. Even as a kid I would throw stone after stone in the pond near our house. And nothing, just a plop. On a recent trip to the lake with my family, I stood on the rocky shore, watching the water come in and out, nearly licking the tops of my shoes. I heard that familiar sound of the plop-plop-plop of a stone bouncing off the top of the water. My husband was skipping stones. And not just two or three little jumps, but three, four, and six even! He had just the right curve to his back and the crook in his arm; complete follow through. It was his skill but also the perfect rocks that he chose. Over and over again he showed off his talent, while I got more and more frustrated that I couldn't do it. Standing back, I watched the kids imitate their father. He helped them choose just the right stone and throw it just the right way. It was a precious scene.

The next morning I ventured out alone. I walked down to that place at the lake where we'd been the day before. Looking at the stones scattered along the shore, I tried to find the perfect one to be my skipping stone. They were different shapes, sizes, and textures. I found what I thought would be the right one. Instead of skipping it, I put it my pocket. I wanted it to be a reminder to me that God sees all of us as His precious gems. He made us. He doesn't just pick one. He picks us all. We are all flawed, but He chooses us anyway! He made us, and in His way we are exactly who we are meant to be. In this morning light I could see clearly.

Our Lord loves us. He loves us more than we can even imagine. It's unconditional. Through our faithfulness, He grants us His mercy.

*F*ather, thank You for Your unending love. We thank You for Your mercy. Count us among Your stones, just right for the picking. Place in us Your Holy Spirit that we may become all that You want and desire of us. Bring us to You, Lord, through Your specific calling, that we may continue to honor and praise You in Your name. We love You. *A*men.

"Grace is nothing else but a certain beginning of glory within us."
St. Thomas Aquinas

"A cheerful glance brings joy to the heart; good news invigorates the bones." Proverbs 15:30

*I*t seems the waistband is tightening up again. With all the running around I do all day long and the work outs I try to incorporate into my day, why doesn't the scale cooperate with my efforts? It couldn't be the hot dog I had for lunch or the birthday cake I nearly inhaled. Could it? Surely not.

I am blessed to live with a man who has his eye on the prize. He is so health conscious and aware, I can't help but take some of his motivation and store it up for myself. It's still hard though, with so many tasty temptations around every corner. The summer time parties scream great food! And how about ice cream on a hot day! Sometimes it's just too much! All of these things are probably OK in moderation. We've all heard it: Moderation, exercise, and healthy eating will lead to a healthy body and healthy lifestyle.

Our Christian lives can be related in much the same way. With so many sinful temptations around every corner, it can be difficult to stay on the path of Christ. We can be surrounded by people who have less than perfect intentions for our well being. Judging ourselves against their behaviors and actions is only going to lead to trouble. That's why it's important to surround yourself with like-minded people. Christian people. People who can bring you up, not take you down. And that can be hard, too. It is easier to sink to a certain immoral level than to bring others up to yours.

Feast on the Word of God. He has more than enough to fill our hearts and souls. And teach others His truth. Don't be afraid to be a witness to his love. You may find it's easier than you think. And put the chocolate away!

God, thank You for who You are. Thank You for lighting the flame within my soul. Help me to gather Your flock and show Your light within me, that I may lead others to know You. Help me to be strong against temptation and call You out by name when I need Your Spirit. I love You. Amen.

"Cast yourself into the arms of God and be very sure that if He wants anything of you, He will fit you for the work and give you strength."
St. Philip Neri

"Hope deferred makes the heart sick, but a wish fulfilled is a tree of life." Proverbs 13:12

Dear Jesus,

I want to continue to get to know You through Your Word and Your Church. I vow to make more time for prayer, reflection and Your sacraments and to share the Good News.

Love,
Christine

I was digging through the kitchen junk drawer yesterday and found this little note. Yes, I have a junk drawer in my kitchen, too! Not just my closet! I must sound like a terrible cluttered mess. Don't ask. But I digress.

About six months ago, I was evaluating my own spiritual life and asking myself what I wanted. How was I going to make the leap from where I was to where I wanted to be? So I sat down and wrote this little note to Jesus. I put it in a "safe" place in hope of being able to look upon it again to see if I had really been able to grow in the way that I had wanted to.

Are you where you want to be right now, spiritually? Is there an emptiness in you that longs to be filled? Or have you become stagnant and need to rev up your faith and praise? What are you waiting for? Establish your own goals of where you want to be and who you want to be. Take a walk with Christ today. Perhaps you can write your own "Dear Jesus" letter, casting all your fears, worries, and ambitions onto Him. Hide it in your special place, only to find it and some day see the glory that He's brought in to your life. Once you decide to walk with Him you will be changed forever.

I love to worship through song. A line from one of my favorite songs says, "What can a poor man lay at the feet of the King?" My answer to this is, "Faith, worship, love and thanksgiving." Sing a love song to the Lord today. Be thankful to Him for holding your life in His hands. Don't wait one more day to live completely within God's love.

*D*ear Jesus, thank You for hearing my intentions. You know what's in my heart. I thank You for Your gentle hand guiding me every step of the way. Although You know I will fall, I know that You will catch me. I want to be in Your love!

*A*men.

"I knew nothing; I was nothing. For this reason God picked me out."

St. Catherine Laboure

"I know indeed how to live in humble circumstances; I know also how to live with abundance. In every circumstance and in all things I have learned the secret of being well fed and of going hungry, of living in abundance and of being in need. I have the strength for everything through Him who empowers me." Philippians 4:12–13

You could have heard a pin drop. The silence; almost deafening, in fact. Not the usual occurrence when I'm hanging with my four children. But this time was different. Instead of watching shows or wrestling for the last cookie or whining about "yucky" dinner, we went to our parish church. We went to pray and just be still. Sometimes I lack the creativity of bridging the gap between the fun day and bedtime. So we spent some much needed time just in silence in the presence of the Lord. I want to teach my children that they can pray and be with Him outside of the mass. Although He's always in our home it's wonderful to be a visitor in His.

Have you ever found yourself saying things like, "If I was just a little thinner . . .," or "If I had more money . . .," or "I wish my house was bigger," or "I wish my house was smaller." I have said all of these things and more. We all have. But what is the point to all of these queries, complaints, or excuses? Why do we feel like what we have isn't enough or good?

Taking a self evaluation of our lives can be extremely eye opening. If you can counter any of the statements with a positive, more "other side of the coin" attitude, would it look a little different? I think so. My dad introduced this to me a long time ago. I'm thankful for the perspective he instilled in me.

The real truth is not looking at what we don't have but rejoicing in what we do have. And being ever so thankful that the Lord has placed us exactly where we are meant to be. We are where we are, and are who we are, because of His glory. There is a teaching moment in everything we experience, every moment. Seizing those moments of truth will lead us to Him. We will see ourselves and others the way God sees us. We can be happy in all things. We can be humble and grateful. Always.

𝒟earest Father in Heaven, we thank You for the moments that take our breath away and for the times that we need the gentle shove to remind us of who we really are. Thank You for the many blessings You've given us, warm friends and a generous family. Please help us to see the good and to be grateful in all circumstances. There are always two sides to every coin. 𝒜men.

"Those whose hearts are pure are the temples of the Holy Spirit."
St. Lucy

"Once more will He fill your mouth with laughter, and your lips with rejoicing." Job 8:21

𝒥 feel like singing today! The sun is shining and so is the SON! You can sing along with me if you'd like. I close my eyes, just before sinking into prayers and before I fall asleep. I thank God for my husband, my kids, my family and friends, usually in that order, too. And I recognize that without our Saving Lord I truly don't know where I'd be.

Just this morning, my toes sunk into the mud beneath me as I walked my garden. To some, that is probably unthinkable and gross. Who would walk around in mud? Me! I love it! It's the closest to heaven I will probably be today. The garden, which happens to be the garden of my soul, is beginning to take on a life of its own. I, its creator, have taken loving care of it. Perhaps in loving it so much, through great excitement and intense anticipation, I was a little over zealous and planted too many vegetables. Just don't tell my father-in-law! The zucchini has taken on a life of its own. Every plant is touching the other. It reminds me of my children when they scream at me, "Mom, he's touching me again!" It makes me laugh. But it's my garden. I can do what I want. A few lessons learned, though.

If it weren't for the puddles in my driveway, I might not have remembered the storm the night before. The breeze this morning held in it the dampness evaporating from the grass, and the gentle pittle, pittle from the dripping leaves was a welcome "good morning."

I pray today that you will find what brings you closest to heaven. Wherever and however you choose to walk, I pray that you find joy and peace. And in all things give thanks! He will fill you with His love. Your lips will sing sweet songs of praise. Like a child, may you bubble with laughter. See the humor of the Lord today and the beauty that He brings to your life. *Amen.*

"Nothing seems tiresome or painful when you are working for a Master who pays well; who rewards even a cup of cold water given for love of Him."

St. Dominic Savio

"No longer shall the sun be your light by day, nor the brightness of the moon shine upon you at night; the Lord shall be your light forever, your God shall be your glory. No longer shall your sun go down, or your moon withdraw, for the Lord will be your light forever, and the days of your mourning shall be at an end."
Isaiah 60:19–20

It creeped. It crawled. It was even suffocating to a point. "It" was me in my own skin. I didn't sleep well last night. Not from bedbugs or the temperature. I had behaved badly and had an ugly disposition with my husband. Then I felt horrible. As much as I regretted the fight I started and as much as I prayed that it would just blow over, it didn't; not at that moment anyway. Sometimes we need to feel it so that we don't repeat it. These lessons are the hardest.

So this morning the sadness and ugliness hung over my head like a dark rain cloud. It followed me all day long. Until . . . I decided to plant some more flowers and mow the lawn. I usually leave the latter to my husband, but I felt I needed to exert some energy and spend some time talking to God amid the hum of the mower. Up and down, in not so straight lines across the yard I walked. And I talked to God. I even cried a little. But it was a good thing; cleansing, in fact. It was then that I was reminded of my humanity. I fail. I disappoint. I get discouraged. Then I dust myself off and vow to do better, to be better.

Remember no matter how ugly or long the night might be, or how difficult the obstacles may seem by day's light, God is there for you. Loving you and forgiving you. Through His merciful love, we can overcome. Go to Him.

Dearest Lord, thank You for being my friend today.
Amen.

"You are children of eternity. Your immortal crown awaits you, to reward your duty and love. You may indeed sow here in tears, but you may be sure there to reap in joy." St. Elizabeth Ann Seton

---

"I am the gate. Whoever enters through Me will be saved, and will come in and go out and find pasture." John 10:9

At last, the house is quiet. I can finally get the dishes done. I can listen to my "Jesus music." I can . . . oh wait! The house isn't supposed to be this quiet, I am reminded, because there are actually three little people home with me. When a house with three small children is quiet, you know something probably just isn't right. As the great mom detective that I am, I quietly peak into the bedrooms: nothing. The basement: nothing again. Then the shrill of laughter floods my ears. It's coming from outside the front door. As I peek out the dining room window, I hear the familiar sound of the hose running. Then I see the three of them delighting in its cool wetness. They've created a waterfall by putting the hose in the tree. This looks like fun. And they are having it. The only problem I see with this is that the "waterfall" is flooding my flower gardens! The plants look as if they will float away with the mulch that is now pooling on my sidewalk. Here's decision time. Do I yank the fun and also ruin my sweet solitude? or do I sacrifice the beds? Perhaps a little of both. I'm patient and take joy in watching them happily play together. As I turn to walk back to the kitchen, a little knock, knock at the front door turns me around.

I open the door. I am the gate keeper standing in front of three wet kids. Smiles from ear to ear, their twinkling eyes barely visible beneath their bangs that should have been trimmed at least a month ago. Trying to hide my own smile, I look them up and down; head to toe. They don't know I've been watching them out the window. You see, now they are cold and would like to prance through the house, bringing with them half my garden on their feet. The smiles turn into half frowns when I ask them what they've been up to. They are surprised and delighted that I'm not angry and as they strip at the door, dry off, and put clothes on. I hug and kiss them each on their wet foreheads.

I wonder if this is how it will be when I show up at those beautiful pearly gates when I'm 90-something (I'm an optimist). I'll get there, smiling ear to ear, all excited to come on in and start my new life. And God will say to me, "Whoa. Wait a minute, missy. What have you been up to all these years?" As if He doesn't know. I will welcome being "stripped at the door and dried," purged of the remnants of my sins. And then, He too, like the loving Father He is, will hug me and welcome me into His arms and His Kingdom.

Dear Lord, thank You for Your goodness and for being the loving Father that You are. I know that You are no farther away than a simple whisper in a prayer. I am Your child and I love You. *Amen.*

"Have you begun to stop trying to defend your sins? Then you have made a beginning of righteousness." St. Augustine of Hippo

"When you call Me, when you go to pray to Me, I will listen to you. When you look for Me, you will find Me." Jeremiah 29:12–13

My first dog was a beagle named Julie. She had about 20 litters of puppies and resembled a pot-bellied pig for as long as I can remember her. What a sweet dog. Being as big as she was, I was always still surprised when she'd show up at the door with a rabbit in her mouth. Our cat, Patches, had a deflated momma belly that nearly dragged on the ground when she walked. I think this was before Bob Barker preached, "Spay and neuter your pets!" Such is life in a small town.

My little posse made up of Julie and Patches would follow me on my paper route. It was rare to see me without them. Imagine, me, a 12-year-old lugging papers about 20 or more steps ahead of the dog, and the cat about 10 paces behind the dog. It's a scene out of a movie or a Kodak moment, at least.

Daily I'd deliver from one end of the town to the other. One of my stops was the nursing home planted on the main street hill. I'd enter in through the lower doors. My crew would stop there at my insistence. After my deliveries and hellos were made, I'd exit the opposite side, at the top, finishing up my paper route and coming back down the other side of the street. Looking over at the nursing home, I would see my faithful followers. Shouting out to them, I'd say, "Yoo-hoo, I'm over here." I'd get this look and almost a double take, as if it were hard to believe that they left me in one spot and I appeared in another. They would shrug their shoulders, as only a cat and dog can do, and trot across the street to join me on the walk home. Another day well done!

There are many moments and many days when I feel like God and I are walking hand in hand, and other times when I actually feel like I've checked Him at the door. I go through these days feeling lost and wondering why it's so hard. Loneliness sets in. Temptation picks at me. And then I hear that sweet, friendly, loving voice calling me back: "Yoo-hoo, I'm over here!" I know who is calling me home. Again, I am found. When I am in a place that I don't want to be, I turn to my bible or to the saints. Every word provides a map that takes me home—home to God's love. If you are lost, pray, "Come Holy Spirit . . .," pick up the great book, open it to a spot and just start reading. Reflect on the passages and bring it into your heart. Each word will bring you closer to Him.

*L*ord, thank You for Your love. Thank You for calling me back. Help me to walk in the light of Your love. *A*men.

"May I not come before You with empty hands, since we are rewarded according to our deeds."
St. Teresa of Avila

"Look to God that you may be radiant with joy and your faces may not blush for shame." Psalms 34:5–6

*H*ow do you feel about yourself when bad thoughts creep in? Or when you start to gossip? Or how about when you fight with those you love? I don't know about you but when I feel unlovely, it is so disappointing. I feel like I've not only let myself down, but God as well. I ask myself if I'm a hypocrite. I wonder how I can seem to be one kind of person and then be someone I don't recognize all in the same hour. Why is that?

I have almost an out-of-body experience at times. I actually can see and hear myself and think, "I need to stop this!" But for some reason, I don't. What's left behind is my guilty, broken heart and, of course, the damage I've done with my words. It is then that, thankfully, I've trained myself to seek forgiveness and ask that God help me stop myself in the future, so that through His love and grace I may find it in me as well.

*F*ather, thank You for forgiving me when I'm not so lovely. For being that whisper in my ear that reminds me of who I really want to be. Allow me to only serve You. *A*men.

"In all talking and conversation let something always be said of spiritual things, and so shall all idle words and evil speaking be avoided."
St. Teresa of Avila

"My strength, Your praise I will sing; You, God, are my fortress, my loving God." Psalms 59:18

Back and forth I've been driving from my home to a friend's home to watch their little doggy. Each time dragging along my little people who love to play with him. And each drive over there has been the same: excitement over seeing this furry friend, kid music blaring through the speakers, and ultimately the arguing which ensues over who's touching who. Now I know that God's dreams for me outnumber the granules of sand on a beach. If only the amount of patience He's given me were equal to that. Sometimes it's just too much to take.

I've driven on this road so many times I could do it in my sleep. Like the days I've been having, it, too, is getting boring and dull. I noticed a left turn that until today has been skipped over. Blinker on, I decided to take it. Hoping it would lead me to where I wanted to be. In a moment I was in a different place, away from the subdivisions and traffic lights. Although I've never been down this road, it had a nostalgic feel to it. The windows down, sunroof open, streams of sunlight poked through the trees overhead. Amazingly enough, the kids quieted in the back seat; nothing but the wind in our faces. In the silence we could hear the birds. Old houses nestled in the woods along the road, although inhabited, seemed to escape being updated. The surrounding land was untouched and undeveloped. I was driving in the country not a block off the main drag. It was exactly what we needed: just a moment to take a breath and be quiet; a moment to feel God's peace and see His beauty. My family calls me a country bumpkin at heart. I think I am. I can't explain the serenity that overtakes me when I'm in this place of nature. It's almost indescribable.

All too quickly, the road came to an end. But as I had hoped, it ended exactly where I needed to be. Turns out, it was a short cut. And so a trip off the beaten path served me well and was a respite for my weary soul.

In a moment, God's whisper, telling me to turn left, became the best part of my day. I plan on visiting often.

Take that road less traveled. Beg your guardian angel to help you hear His voice. Listen to the slightest of His whispers. You'll be glad you did. He knows what you need and when.

Heavenly Father, thank You for allowing me to hear You. Thank You for knowing me so well that I am led to You through the smallest of things. I am thankful for all that You are. Please continue to fill me with Your grace today as I try to be everything that You want me to be. I pray that others are able to see Your face in me. I love You.   Amen.

"I pray God may open your eyes and let you see what hidden treasures He bestows on us in the trials from which the world thinks only to flee."   St. John of Avila

---

"As for me and my household, we will serve the Lord."
Joshua 24:15

Fluorescent lights in the dressing room. Don't you love 'em? Hate them! I think that's probably the reason I don't like to shop for clothing. The light hits all of the wrong parts in all of the wrong ways. Nothing looks good in there. And shopping for a new bathing suit, in my book, is just plain torture! And the tale begins:

"Leave me alone!" "Get out of here!" "Don't look at me! You stupid head!" Yes, these are my children playing in the dressing room stalls while I am trying on a bathing suit. I take a deep breath as I rush to get the top and bottom on quickly before they climb under my door and tell me everything that's wrong with my body, as if I don't already know. Kids are good at that. Their squabbling didn't bother me much because, as I said, they hadn't gotten to me yet, but the last insult is what caught my attention. Immediately I corrected her and told her that we don't say those things in our family. She whispered to the other suspect, " Man, she hears everything!" And to that I then heard, "Yeah. She prayed to God that she would be able to see and hear everything we do. And He listened!"

I try to be a model to my children by teaching them what God expects from us as Christians. Bringing His love and law into our homes is essential in our personal growth, too. Creating a loving and God-loving environment is a key ingredient to a happy life and home. It's not about guilt or fear, necessarily. It's about the love and respect for ourselves and others, which ultimately is serving the Lord.

Showing Christ's love for yourself will radiate to others as well. Not just our core family, but it reaches further than that; to friends, extended family, and strangers. Being a witness as to how Christ is in our lives brings others closer to Him. Who wouldn't want to be filled with so much joy and love? Who wouldn't also want to be contagious with the greatest of strength and grace? They'll say, "Give me some of that!" That is how Christ's love works. He enters the hearts and homes of His most faithful followers. He leads us to the kingdom first in knowing that we will lead others.

Be a light, a gateway if you will, for others to be led. Radiate your own peace and love for our Lord today.

Dear Lord, thank You for the love You give to me. Take the grace and beauty and strength You've given me and help me to use it as a tool to guide those who have not yet come to You. Help them to feel Your love today and to see Your presence in every glorious thing. For You are great! You are holy! And You are loved! *A*men.

"First let a little love find entrance into their hearts, and rest will follow."
St. Philip Neri

"This is my commandment: Love one another as I love you. No one has greater love than this, to lay down one's life for one's friends." John 15:12–13

"*T*hat hitted the spot!" said my five-year-old rootbeer float aficionado. Not unlike the swirling and sniffing of a fine wine, so, too, must the foam be slurped, leaving behind a mustache; the ice cream crunchy like ice shavings reduced from the soda. MMM . . . cool and yummy. And I agreed, it hitted the spot.

Not long ago I was preparing for a visit from my "besty," all the while reminding myself to be a Mary and not a Martha. While running around doing laundry, dusting and vacuuming, I realized I wasn't having any fun and neither were the kids. So I plunked them in the car and we drove across town to get that rootbeer float (and some onion rings!). Going didn't take much more than a decision to do so. I love anticipating the coming of a good friend, but I can get caught up in the preparation. Not only that, I neglect the little people I love, shoving their comments and cares to the side. Summer time is one of my favorite seasons, and it can go by all too fast.

My friend arrived later that day and spent two wonderful, but short, days with me. We visited over coffee on my front step, trading seats both mornings to get a different view of the flowers. She dabbled in my fountain the way I do every morning. It was so nice to look into her blue eyes and see the crease of her smile as we talked. We shared a lot in those two days: laughter, silly secrets, concerns, and plans for our upcoming vacation.

I was asked who my best friend was the other day by my daughter. I explained that I have lots of best friends, all special to me in different and unique ways. I started with my husband and went on from there. My husband was asked the same question and without hesitation, he answered, "Mommy."

Having friends, making them, and keeping them is a wonderful blessing. I pray that you are able to experience this gift from above as well. Recognize those whom you love and make them your "besty." And be thankful for their presence in your life. I am.

*D*ear Father, thank You for the loving relationships I hold so dear to my heart. Thank You for allowing those I love to continue to shape me as Your child. I am so thankful for my best friends—my husband, my children, my family, and friends, in that order—and for You, heavenly Father, for Your care and love. Please humble me and help me to accept my faults with grace and to live up to the expectation You present to me daily. I long to live in Your light. *Amen.*

"Take God for your spouse and friend and walk with Him continually, and you will not sin and will learn to love, and the things you must do will work out prosperously for you."

St. John of the Cross

"The Lord is with me to the end. Lord, Your love endures forever. Never forsake the work of your hands!" Psalms 138:8

"Just Do It." Very straight forward. Simple. So I did. I got on my running shoes and hit the treadmill. Didn't particularly want to, but I did. It's very important to me to maintain a healthy weight and an attractive physique. I try. I do my best every day to eat the right foods and do the right amount of exercise. Right now I'm trying to incorporate weight training. I have an awesome coach and mentor. But no matter how much you lead a horse to water, you can't make him drink. But again, I do my best.

Exercise is the preventive maintenance we do to achieve a healthy body and to ward off illness and injury, even trying to postpone feeling old and helpless. We worry so much about this body and this life. What if we put as much energy into our spiritual life? Isn't it worth investing in that body and life, too? Not only to help us now but what about after our bodies are gone and all that's left is our spirit? Feeding ourselves with the Word of God, incorporating His grace into our lives and exercising His teachings to others is the preventive maintenance and the regimen that will ensure our everlasting life, not just the life as we know it now.

Is there any better time than now to "Just Do It"? I can't imagine waiting another moment or another day. We aren't promised tomorrow, or even another hour for that matter. Go to your Heavenly Father. Ask Him for help in getting you started. Claim Him as your Savior. And thank Him for allowing Him to enter your heart and lead you to Him. It's as simple as opening a page in the bible. My favorite place to start when I've fallen off the wagon, and I do, is the book of Matthew. Start from the beginning. Just Do It!

Dear God, I am thankful for the strength You give me every day. I am thankful that I know how to come to You. Thank You for loving me as I am, faults and all. I ask that You continue to fill me with Your Spirit. Thank You for being my friend whom I can turn to in need. Unlike this earthly body, my love for You will last forever. Amen.

"God did not tell us to follow Him because He needed our help, but because He knew that loving Him would make us whole."

St. Irenaeus of Lyons

"The heavens declare the glory of God; the sky proclaims its builder's craft. One day to the next conveys that message; one night to the next imparts that knowledge." Psalms 19:2–3

I'm taking names today. Who told the deer I was on vacation? You know the saying 'while the cat's away, the mice will play.' Well, in this case the deer had a party in my yard. Everything is gone. They even jumped the fence in my veggie garden and got to the tomato plants. There's really nothing to say about it. I guess I could feel like my entire spring and partial summer have been a waste of time and energy. But I could also feel happy and blessed for what I did get out of it for the time I was able to spend grooming the vegetables and flowers. Now all that remain are tall stems plucked of flowers and stripped of leaves: pitiful. But oh well. There is more time to be spent on other things, like enjoying the rest of our summer. Today I am delighting in being home. I am basking in the memories of a wonderful time with my family. And I am ever so thankful for safe travels.

May your love for God reach others in ways you aren't aware of today. And may you feel His loving arms around you, holding you and loving you in the ways you need it the most today. May He give rest to your weary body, mind and heart.

Dearest Lord, thank You for Your glory. Thank You for Your love. Please extend Your loving hand to me and all who reach for You today. Show us Your grace and mercy and pour forth Your love that we may be filled with joy. Amen.

"He who loses an opportunity is like the man who lets a bird fly from his hand, for he will never recover it." St. John of the Cross

---

"I will praise you, Lord, with all my heart; I will declare all Your wondrous deeds. I will delight and rejoice in You; I will sing hymns to Your name, Most High." Psalms 9:2–3

Sitting down at the kitchen table, dishing out some fantastic cuisine (I made it!), most of the faces were happy. They were wide eyed as I took the lid off of the casserole dish, tummies rumbling, forks in hand, eagerly awaiting the spoonful of yumminess that was about to embark on their plates. All but one little cherub was happy. My sweet little booboos sat there, nose scrunched, smile upside-down, arms crossed. He was also sitting in just his little Underoos. Knowing that he was not about to eat "our" dinner, I quickly made his favorite blue box pasta. Yeah, the really good stuff! As I dished it, dad said to him, "So you get something different. Do you think you're special?" And to his question came the sweetest of responses, "Mom thinks I am." Talk about melting my heart! "Oh, of course I know you're special," I confirmed.

I have been extremely inconsistent in my reflections and devotions lately, partly because I have had my daily routine ravaged by summer vacation, but really it's probably from laziness and lack of discipline . What I am grateful for, however, is that God very lovingly and subtly brings me back each time. He shows me that although I may get side tracked a bit, He is still here waiting for me. I know that I need do nothing more than to go to Him in prayer, asking for forgiveness for turning a cold shoulder, however brief it has been, and ask Him to welcome me back. And thank Him for His love and patience with me.

Establishing a good routine every day allows time for some of the most important things in our lives. Mass (if at all possible), prayer and reflection should be at the top of those priorities. Can we really get through the day without our praise to Our Lord? Isn't life really about more than just getting through the day? I forget that sometimes. I forget that this life is fleeting and that it is my eternal life I am preparing for. My soul depends on what I do right now. Today. Preventive maintenance, if you like.

Today, make a promise to yourself and to God that you will come to Him daily; that you will make time for Him. Don't let yourself get so far away that it feels difficult to come back or that you've lost your way.

Dearest God, thank You for being right here, by my side. Just as You always are. I ask You to please forgive me for being led astray. My heart was feeling empty, but now it is full again. Please humble me in Your presence, fill me with Your grace, love and joy. I ask You, Lord, to help me reflect those qualities to others that they may be led to You. Please bless our families, friends, and those we haven't yet met. Keep them and all in Your loving care. Amen.

"Control your tongue and your belly." St. Anthony the Great

"In the same way, the Spirit, too, comes to the aid of our weakness; for we do not know how to pray as we ought, but the Spirit itself intercedes with inexpressible groanings. And the one who searches hearts knows what is the intention of the Spirit, because it intercedes for the holy ones according to God's will. We know that all things work for good for those who love God, who are called according to His purpose." Romans 8:26–28

It was another morning when my brain started working well before my eyes were ready to be open. But as I lay in bed, still snug as a bug, my heart began beating faster, my breathing more shallow and not as relaxed as when I lay in deep sleep. I stumbled to the kitchen, pouring my "mama juice" (coffee; not to be mistaken) and perched myself in my usual spot on the front step. Staring out at the stubble of a garden that rested before me, I could still hear the frogs and crickets, even an owl. It was definitely earlier than I had anticipated being awake. The sprinklers spouted out, adding their own music to the morning. And the scent on the wind was that of sweet, wet grass.

Sitting there, I reflected on something an acquaintance had remarked on the day before. When I mentioned that I was the mom of a 15-year-old, she said that I looked too young to have a child that old. I was young when I had her; 20, in fact. My reflection this morning was about the feelings I had during that time in my life that seems so far away now. I don't recall feeling nervous or scared. I didn't worry about much more than satisfying her immediate needs. I never thought twice about my decision to be a mom unexpectedly, either. I just knew it would be OK. That's how we started our lives together. One day at a time. I won't say that every day was easy or always filled with joy. But I've never looked back or regretted anything.

If there's one thing I try to instill in my children, it's the fact that they are loved no matter what and that through any circumstance we can make it through together, just as my parents taught me. I share with my children that I have wishes for them. Wishes that they will abstain from risky behavior, work hard in school, and nourish their friendships. And that at every happy heart is your home, family and God.

I didn't know that God was at the center of my being during my early days of being a mom. But I know that He was. How else could I have made it through? How else would I be here today with a loving husband and four beautiful children? I still don't worry about tomorrow. But unlike yesterday, I have a very clear picture of who's in charge and who's by my side. And I know that on the days when I can only sigh or groan, He knows what I need.

I pray that you can look at the details of your life and see how God was present for you, even and especially the most difficult of times. I pray that you give thanks for His tender mercies and His grace that has most certainly filled your days and nights in ways you may not even recognize yet.

Dearest Lord, thank You for knowing me so well. Thank You for knowing how I need You and when. Thank You also for coming along for the good times, as any friend is happy to do. I love You. *Amen.*

"Seeing God means following Him wherever He might lead."
St. Gregory of Nyssa

"Learn to savor how good the Lord is; happy are those who take refuge in him." Psalms 34:9

Sleeping bags: check. Flashlights: check. Tent: big check! Camping and traveling for the most part this summer has eluded me. Busy and summer are not two words I usually put together. Sure, we always do fun stuff but not because we have to, but because we love to. This year has been different. With children entering new seasons of their lives, about to enter high school and kindergarten, much has been done to ready them. And not to forget about the twins in between, who have fallen in love with the idea of sleep-overs and friend dates. And of course a mom eager to continue to find herself and her place in all of this while staying focused on the Truth. And a dad just trying to keep up with us. We are just too busy.

Well, this camping thing is definitely a realty for us all now. We are about to embark on a trip of a life time. My cherubs and I and my besty and her son are going on a huge cross-country camping trip. When all is said and done, we will be gone for 17 days. We are sure to experience many highs and hopefully limited lows on our trip. We are as prepared as we think we can be.

You can be sure that God will be guiding our adventure, protecting us, and watching over us. Because of His goodness we have been blessed with this friendship. We have been blessed with a sense and a desire to enjoy life and to bring our children along for the ride.

I pray for those we will be leaving behind that their days are filled with light and happiness. I pray to our dear Lord to bless them all with joy and safety. I pray for continued love and to be filled with the grace of God; not only to enjoy today, but to rejoice in every day. That He will humble me in His sight.

A good friend of mine talked to me about being blessed with a huge heart. He said that when we have huge hearts, not only do we feel more, but we hurt more. It is a blessing, not a weakness, to consider others before ourselves. Because of this, sometimes we may hurt. But ultimately it is the love that keeps us going. So I implore you to continue to love and continue to care and take risks, even if it means you may be hurt. God has created you the way you are for a reason and to His likeness. He will replace any voids and any hurt with His love.

*D*earest Father in Heaven, thank You for Your love. Thank You for the friendships we hold so dear to our hearts. Thank You for giving me a heart so big that it hurts sometimes. Please bless all who have gathered on this page. Continue to bring them closer to You through Your Word and Your truth! We rejoice in Your name. *A*men.

"Thinking is a new, inward knowing, with great reverence and loving awe."

St. Julian of Norwich

"Every valley shall be filled and every mountain and hill shall be made low. The winding roads shall be made straight and the rough ways be made smooth, and all flesh shall see the salvation of God." Luke 3:5–6

"Knock, Knock."

"I'm busy, come back later!"

"Knock, Knock."

"I know. I'll get back with you later!"

"Knock! Knock! Anyone there? Why aren't you answering?"

I wish this was the beginning of one of those cute little jokes my kids dig out of a knock, knock book, but sadly, it's not. It's God speaking directly to me. Searching for me. Wondering where I've gone.

Crrreeeek. The door opens. The thin, almost invisible string of webs runs across my face and sticks to my cheeks and hair. It's been a while since this door has opened.

Suddenly, from nowhere I hear the faint tune from an old western movie; Clint Eastwood, perhaps. You know the windy whistle as a tumble weed blows over his boots?

Such was the scene as I stepped onto my deck after returning from vacation. Sticks replaced my beautiful flowers that once overflowed their pots. Their plump, green leaves, now only crunchy debris, lay at my feet. The love of my life forgot to water my flowers while I was away. They were screaming at me, "Where have you been!"

And so, without delay, I picked the dead. I watered the dry. I reshaped the remaining foliage. With time and attention, my once waste land of a potted garden is lush again with smooth green leaves and bursting with color. Fragrant blooms now replace those same sticks that just a week ago offered little beauty and no satisfaction.

Today I have opened my bible for the first time in a while, too. The Word jumped out at me and reignited a spark that had turned into barely a flicker.

Lately my road has seemed long and winding, bumpy, and even scary. I have felt alone, betrayed, anxious, nervous; you name it and I have felt it. I have felt misunderstood. I have also felt deep, wonderful love and God's peace.

What is ever so amazing to me is that when I seemingly turned my back and allowed myself to get caught up in small, insignificant moments, God knew how to pull me back. He planted just the right people and signs in my life to bring me back. I have never stopped praying or being thankful, but I can look back over the past month and see myself as the window gardener. I have been watching my flowers, hoping for rain and yet not doing anything to nourish or care for them. Much is the same for my spirituality lately. I've prayed. I've asked others to pray for me, But never opened my book. Never got down on my own two knees. Well, no more!

I'm getting my hands dirty again! Diving back into that garden, pulling those weeds. I'm going to fertilize my own spiritual growth by digging into my bible and rediscovering God's truth. And it feels so good to be back!

Heavenly Father, thank You as always for bringing me back through Your door. Help me please to be an instrument of Your peace and love. Thank You for the gifts You've given me. I pray that I am made worthy through them to be presented to You. I thank You for calling me to Your kingdom and all those who believe and trust in Your divinity. Though the road is rough, we know it is made easier through our love in You. You smooth the edges. We know You. We trust You and we love You. Amen.

"Virtue is nothing but well-directed love." St. Augustine of Hippo

---

"He did not doubt God's promise in unbelief; rather he was empowered by faith and gave glory to God and was fully convinced that what he had promised he was also able to do."
Romans 4:20–21

Sweat dripping from my brow, I wiped it away with the back side of my dirty palm. You guessed it. I'm back in the yard again. The vegetables are spent, the marigolds, having seen

better days, have served this garden well, protecting my harvest from the rabbits. The cool evenings and warm afternoons provide an ideal state to plant the mums and pansies.

Fatigued and dizzy, my sweet brown-eyed little boy approaches me with a drink to quench my thirst. (Is this sounding familiar? Keep reading.) I thank him, because I know he only does things from his heart. Taking a long gulp of cool water from his over-sized red water bottle, I am touched at how kind my child is to me; to see I'm tired and thirsty and offering me a drink. Here it comes: "Mom, there's all sorts of germs on that." and he smiles. "Huh? Say what?" I groan. You may recall the time he brought me out a glass of cold, soapy bath water from earlier that morning? Yeah. Can someone please tell me why I continue to accept drinks from this kid? Pray for me! I still don't know what he meant by "all sorts of germs," but I am sure that will be a story for another day.

It might be September, but the sun feels just as high some days as it was in July. It would seem that the Wisconsin girl in me is still on the fall schedule of it being normally cool this time of year. Not so where I live. But none the less, I have the mums in the ground, gourds on the front step, and pumpkins on my walkway. A new wreath hangs on the front door. I really couldn't be more pleased with the appearance of my front yard. Looking from the street, it seems very neat, orderly, pretty, and somewhat well planned. It would also appear that the deer have migrated to a new neighborhood. Not really. I've just been more diligent in my flower preservation objective.

Not unlike the appearance of my front yard, I fear that I, too, have put on a good face recently. Applying make up once in a while, putting on a dress, even doing my hair (not every day as that would be crazy!), I have been able to give the impression of being all together, neat, orderly and pleased or happy or content. But underneath all of that I have felt somewhat lost and distracted. Lost from the Truth.

Imagine standing in a dark hallway with nothing on either side, only darkness. A dimly lit doorway stands in front of you. Knocking, it is hollow. Slowly the door creeks open; open to absolutely nothing. Nothing but space. No sunshine. No music. No birds. No flowers. Nothing.

Reaching out in front of me, I cry, "Lord where are you? Why can't I feel the warmth that so usually completes me? Why am I missing You? Why aren't You there!"

At mass this past Sunday, this image came to me once again. Tears flowed during Amazing Grace as it became clear to me. It wasn't I who was standing at the door knocking, waiting for God. It was God, Himself, tapping on my heart, wondering where I was. Why have I been distracted? When was I coming back? It came full circle, and the spot light was on me. At that moment, I knew my days were going to be brighter. Sometimes there are no tangible reasons why we drift away from God. Or why we feel lonely. Maybe we're lonely because we've drifted? I do know, though, that the face I now wear reflects what's truly in my heart. No more pretending and trying to hold it together. I feel together. I am together.

In my cries to Jesus, asking Him to make a way for me, He showed me that He never left. When I was the loneliest inside, that is when He was there the most. He and I have never felt closer.

I am most blessed by my dearest friends, family and my closest, most loving friend, my husband. I can ask for no more, but to be one with God. And by His grace and mercy, all the days will be full of sunshine, happiness and joy. May you have faith in our Lord that He will perform wondrous works within your heart and that you feel His love today.

*D*earest God, thank You for the crosses I carry in this life that bring me ever closer to You, day by day. Forgive me in my weakness and fill me with the strength that can only come from loving You. *A*men.

"God loves each of us as if there were only one of us."

St. Augustine of Hippo

"And He asked them, 'But who do you say that I am?' Peter said to Him in reply, 'You are the Messiah.'" Mark 8:29

It's the Great Pumpkin Patch, Charlie Brown! Is it time to get out in the pumpkin fields yet? I can't hardly wait. Sure, I've purchased mine at the store, but it's not quite fall until you take a hay ride out on the farm and pick your own.

I have always been in love with this season. Maybe because it's my birthday or maybe it's the way the leaves turn magnificent colors, crackling under my feet and a light wind carrying on it the scent of a wood burning stove. And the apples! And cider! Oh my!

There's a lot of consideration that goes into picking the right pumpkin. Do you choose the lumpy one with a flat side? Or the one so big you need to roll it back to the tractor? Or maybe it's the little one with the curled handle. Funny, because really, they're all the same on the inside: pulp and seeds.

Thinking back to grade school, I remember a girl in my class who called me names all the time. Whenever I'd answer a question asked by the teacher, she'd look at me and say, "You're so stupid." It didn't matter if I had the answer right or not. I remember how that made me feel inside: Stupid for one, insecure, shy and sad, to name a few more. I allowed that girl to define who I was. Her words reverberated in my head for years, forcing me to define myself by what she told me I was. And now, being an adult, it often isn't any easier. There have been times when I've been called other names just as hurtful. And questioning myself, I wonder if I, again, allow that to define me.

Christ sees the lovely and the beautiful in us. If we believe in Christ's love and that He is the Messiah, we are called to be as He is. Beauty and loveliness. Because of this, we too must see the beauty and grace in others. So when a hurtful name or remark comes our way, we can be certain that not only did it not come from Christ, but that the person who said this to us is not, at that moment, one with Christ, either. What other explanation is there? When you are walking with Him, you are able to see His light in the eyes of others. What appear to be weaknesses are simply what makes them unique.

Define yourself by the light of Christ that shines in you. Take the compliments and the remarks to heart of those who walk with Him. That is the true measure of your being.

I think this year I'm going to find the lumpiest, most oddly shaped pumpkin I can find. Maybe one without a handle even; like me, a little rough, a little odd. I don't always have a handle on everything, but on the inside I'm the same as everyone else: a heart and a soul.

*D*earest Jesus, thank You for making a way for me today. Please bless all of my special friends and bring them into Your light. We know we won't be perfect. We just ask You to help us bring something special to the world and allow others to see You within us. *A*men.

"No man truly has joy unless he lives in love." St. Thomas Aquinas

---

"And immediately a cock crowed a second time. Then Peter remembered the word that Jesus had said to him. 'Before the cock crows twice you will deny me three times.' He broke down and wept." Mark 14:72

"*T*ake me out to the ball game . . ."

Bases are loaded. It's the bottom of the third! The monkey on the mound winds up his arm and the pitch is good!

The ball hits the side of her foot and goes sailing over third base, not too far out of reach of Dad. Did you think I was talking about baseball? This is better than baseball. It's a family kickball game. Boys against girls, to be exact. I take off in a sprint from second base, determined to be safe at third. As in slow motion, I spot the outfielder (my husband) get the ball. We both know what's at stake here. The theme song to Chariots of Fire begins to play. We both look at third base and then at each other. I fly and then dive into the base, landing on my right shoulder, digging my knee into the ground and then lie there in pain. Beating my husband! I am safe! You know, it's not like when you're a kid. We don't bounce as well as we used to. Celebrating my victory run, I look around for my team mates who should be occupying each of the other two bases. Second base is empty. First base holds two runners. What! All that, and no one ran to second? Seizing the opportunity, my husband creamed the runner and the game is over.

One of my twins was crying this morning. She was made invisible on the playground during a soccer game at recess. It seems this happens often with her. Being a quiet, sensitive girl, she is often the last one picked. She is often forgotten. Not unlike a girl I used to know. It breaks my heart to watch her go through this. I do what I can as a mom to mentor her, to guide her, and to coach her. I involve teachers and counselors when necessary, and I try to build her confidence by getting her involved in sports and clubs that compliment her interests and personality. It's easy to stick up for her. I love her. I can't deny her comfort and protection because not only is she my child, but she also belongs to God. I can't deny her any more than I can deny Him.

So we all know that watching over God's smallest of beings comes easy, but what about the bigger ones? The playground bullies often grow up to be the big bullies we encounter as adults. What do we do when we see or hear someone being abused physically or verbally by another? Do we turn a blind eye and not get involved? Do we stick up for this person and offer cover and protection? What about when the bully is a friend of yours? What do you do when you witness something ugly being done to one of God's children by a friend? How easy is it to stand up to them and make them face their ugliness?

Because we are all God's children, we can deny no one peace and protection. It is our responsibility as Christians to take care of one another. To deny others this love is to deny Christ. Much like Peter, we can be guilty of denying Him through our words, our actions, or just by standing by and doing nothing. The road is rough and the valley is deep. It is made smoother by our faith in Him. Let us love each other as He intended. Deny Him not.

Ugliness is not Christlike. It's something else. Fill yourself, your life, with the goodness that He provides and is intended for you. Surround yourself with those who exude only His love, and watch out for each other. Even when it means standing up to a friend for what is right.

So when the bases are loaded and there are two outs, which way will you go? Will you sprint to home plate with everything you've got? Leaving it all on the field? Will you never look back? Or will you stand by and watch others play out the game?

God is so good. And He wants only the best for His children. May we live up to His promise and honor His gift today. Better people make a better world. Be the difference in someone's life today. Let your light shine!

Dear God, with the heart and faith of a child I come to You today as one of Your littlest ones. Please fill my heart with humility and humble me in the face of others. Allow me the strength to protect the underdogs. Help me to change the ugliness. Fill me with the strength and courage that comes from Your Holy Spirit. *Amen.*

"Laugh and grow strong."   St. Ignatius Loyola

"Yet, O Lord, You are our Father; we are the clay and You the potter; we are all the work of Your hands." Isaiah 64:7

Beep. Beep. Beep. Could it really be time to wake up already? Really? I take a deep breath in and deflate with a sigh. My jammies are tangled around my legs, I trip over my slippers as I fall out of bed, and stumble to find my hair piece and glasses. As if any of these items are going to help me get the day going. It may take more than my usual "cup of ambition" to get this party started. I have a long morning ahead of me: breakfast to prepare, lunches to ready, homework to sign, snacks to provide, animals to feed . . . you get the picture. Oh, and I need to get ready for bible study and bake a quiche! I'm tired just reliving this morning's memories. And this seems to be a rerun I play over and over every day.

One of the girls said to me today that a child on the play ground called her junk. My first instinct was to track down the child's mother! The next, more gentle approach and response was to tell my daughter that God does not make junk. I explained again that God made her and me and many good people I know with a big heart. Because of our big hearts, we feel more and we love more. We also get hurt more. It is a blessing and a cross.

Have you ever felt like junk? Like nothing you do is good enough? Like it isn't enough? How about taking time out for yourself? Time to take a deep breath? Even God rested on the seventh day. And Jesus knew when He had to take a break from healing and teaching. He took a break to pray, to eat, to get rejuvenated. So if Jesus knew when He needed to refill his soul, why do we think that we can do better than that? When we are thirsty, we take a drink.

In a prayer to the Holy Spirit, I asked to be filled with joy, energy and peace today. I asked that I be given enough time to accomplish everything I thought needed to be done. I even started to make a bargain with God, "If you do this, I'll do that." "So unnecessary." That's what I heard Him say back to me. I was told to find the joy within myself and that the peace is already there. And the energy? Well, that comes from within, too. Having a positive attitude, putting my best foot forward. And the time? Well, the time comes from making time for the Lord. Going to Him with prayer and praise. When we make time for the Lord, He will make time for us.

Fluffing yesterday's curls, applying a little lipstick, and throwing together an outfit to drape over my tired shell, I felt uplifted from within by a different spirit than the one I started my morning with.

I heard something inspiring this morning that went to my heart. I heard that God does not make junk. Although we may feel at times as if we're all over the place with random thoughts and misplaced energy or even the very right intentions, we feel a mess. But through the faith that God loves us and He made us, we know we are not junk. We may be a mess. But we are a beautiful mess. Please accept that truth yourself. Realize that, of course, you're not perfect. The day doesn't always go as well as you had hoped. You can't control everything. But you are beautiful. And love yourself for that truth. God does!

Father, You are shaping me daily to be the face and hands of Jesus Christ. Help me to accept my faults and shortcomings.

Thank You for making me beautiful from the inside out.

Amen.

"God is more anxious to bestow His blessings on us than we are to receive them."
St. Augustine of Hippo

"I keep the Lord always before me; with the Lord at my right, I shall never be shaken. Therefore my heart is glad, my soul rejoices; my body also dwells secure." Psalms 16:8–9

Something twinkling from the corner of my eye catches my attention this morning. It's the gentle movement of the leaves outside my cozy spot in front of the window. A fall breeze catches in its path the trees awaiting the brilliance of the colors guaranteed to outfit them this autumn. As sure as I sit here today admiring the green still in their leaves, there will come a day when I will look up again and see the hues of yellow, orange, and red; deep purples, too, and even some browns. And I will wonder, "When did this happen?" Time changes everything. From the new birth of spring flowers and baby shrubs to the maturing maple in all its splendor.

We are changed, too, in time. From new, fresh babies being swaddled by our mothers, to who we are today. Some have traveled a longer, rougher road. Some see the glory and beauty in every precious moment while others struggle to see even a spark.

Pursuing holiness can be rough, even torturous; eliminating distractions and temptations. Yes, there is beauty in salvation, but there is also loneliness at times. 1 Peter 1:15–16 states, "But as He who called you is holy, be holy yourselves, in every aspect of your conduct, for it is written, 'Be holy because I am holy.'" A difficult instruction to follow, at best.

The term martyr comes to mind today. Not in the pious sense of the word, but in the name of grace. Martyr, by Christian definition, is a person who is killed for maintaining a belief knowing that this will almost certainly result in imminent death (without intentionally seeking death). Martyrs sometimes decline to defend themselves at all, in what they see as a reflection of Jesus' willing sacrifice. Talk about a difficult instruction! We may not literally be put to death for standing up for what we believe, but we can feel as though this is happening within our hearts. It happens when we feel misunderstood, when we feel as though we can't share our faith with others. We may want to shout from the roof tops and defend our position. We may want to "make" people understand or "make" them believe in the same. This is not the way. Sometimes, *sometimes,* less is more. Accepting the gift of faith is a cross of its own. You can be a martyr within your own heart by accepting the gift with grace. Live a good example through your actions of kindness and love. 1 Peter 2:18–25 says, "Speak no insult, suffering for doing good is a grace of God."

It's nearly too cold to tiptoe barefoot through the garden now. The tip of my nose is cold, and I can see my breath in the crisp morning air. I pray that the Holy Spirit fills any voids you may have today and that you know you are not carrying your cross alone. You're never truly alone. The closer you get to holiness, the less alone you really are.

"Let your love for one another be intense." 1 Peter 4:8

Dear Father, thank You for this glorious, joyful day. In Your name alone I rejoice. Let Your face shine on Your servant; save me in Your kindness. (Psalms 31:17) Amen.

"The death of the martyrs blossoms in the faith of the living."
St. Pope Gregory the Great

"For with You is the fountain of life, and in Your light we see light." Psalms 36:10

I've been in this chair many times in the last few weeks and I have the bruises on my cheeks to prove it. No not down there!

On my face! I lie in the dentist chair waiting for the torture to begin. The dentist reaches in with his vibrating drill and asks me if I'm OK. I give the thumbs up and he continues.

To the simple spectator I look as calm as a summer breeze: My arms lay on my stomach, hands together, fingers interlocking. My legs are crossed at the ankles. But inside . . . *inside,* I am screaming! Get me outta here! I imagine my legs kicking and arms flailing about. Then I hear my dentist laughing, no—cackling—as he continues to drill. His assistant is actually spraying more water on my face than she's sucking up! Well, thank God for the protective eye wear they gave me! I was wondering what those were for.

You know I feel this way sometimes in my spirituality, too. On the outside, I'm all put together, or not, but I probably don't always reflect exactly what's going on inside. I want to share the Good News with everyone! I want them to know our Savior is born. I want them to know that they can be saved, too! I want them to feel the peace and the grace by which I live. But sometimes I'm afraid. I'm afraid of being judged if I use the common phrases I use with my friends. I'm afraid to answer their complaints with "consider yourself blessed." And so I listen and I pray.

I believe we have all been called to be a witness at all times. That's not to say that it is always easy to do so. More often than not, it's most difficult with the people who know you the best, like your family and close friends. When you've been renewed in the spirit and are awaiting the same for your loved ones, it can feel like a lonely place. And so we must pray. We must pray that we stay strong and that we speak the truth even when it's difficult. Wear your faith on your sleeve. Breathe the words our Lord has given us. Let them comfort and inspire others.

The dentist chair awaits me again today. And when my hands are clenched and fingers locked, you can bet I will be praying.

*D*ear God, thank You for the gift of Your Spirit. Thank You for making me strong in Your love. I will spread Your joy.

*A*men.

"You must refuse nothing you recognize to be His will."

St. Jane Frances de Chantal

"May mercy, peace, and love be yours in abundance." Jude 1:2

On the eve of my 36th birthday, it seems appropriate to take a moment to reflect on yet another year passing. It's raining cats-and-dogs outside now, and the leaves have all nearly faded to yellow and brown. My pooch lays at my feet, snuggling my toes, while I sit with a blanket on my lap. I'm cozy, warm, and safe. The kids will be rushing through the front door soon, hungry and excited to share with me, all at once, the exciting ups and downs of their day. As a mom, I will divide my attention one hundred different ways, not only hearing every word they speak but also caring about each syllable they utter.

I've been on a journey this past year. I've meandered from one side of the road to the other, having a hard time staying straight some days. I've passed through valleys and have soared to the peaks of high, emotional mountains. I've spent moments asking "Why?", "Why not?", and "Surely you don't mean me?" I've had even greater moments of "Thank you Lord!" and "I exalt you!" I've cried in a whisper, "Do unto me Lord. I will follow You no matter what." And I've pleaded, "Be gentle with me today, Lord." And you know, like a good, loving Father, He has heard me. He has divided His attention and cares about all that I proclaim.

I have learned about mercy and forgiveness. I've reflected, most recently, on the times in my life when I have been hurt and how I have reacted. Most often we feel we need to demand forgiveness or demand an apology. The biggest step toward holiness is offering mercy. Giving mercy before it is asked for, forgiving before the apology. Christ died for our sins and forgave us. He died so that we might live. Each day is a new day. I have learned that I don't want to be weighted by a heavy heart, and forgiving and showing mercy are taking steps in the right direction—the Godly direction.

I have a joke about my age, which I think I might be the only one who finds it funny. A while ago, I was 26 and I held onto that for a couple of years. Then I finally turned 28 and stayed there for a while too. I've been 34 now for a bit, and I guess I can admit, at least today, that I will turn 36 tomorrow. I don't know why I hang on to those ages. It's not as if they were any better than where I'm at now. In fact, I feel the most secure and happy right now, today, than I ever have before.

So here's to a new year of miracles and a commitment to making a difference in the lives of others: to be humble, charitable, giving, loving, and merciful.

Dearest Lord, thank You for the life You've given me. Thank You for the mercy You show me every time I fall to my knees. Thank You for the forgiveness and the love You offer. I praise You and I love You.   *Amen.*

"The saints rejoiced at injuries and persecutions, because in forgiving them they had something to present to God when they prayed to Him."   St. Teresa of Avila

---

"I give thanks to my God at every remembrance of you."
Philippians 1:3

It all started with an itch. You know that itch that makes you roll from one side to the other in the wee hours of the morning? And then another itch. This time just enough of an annoyance to get the wheels turning. "Don't look at the clock. Don't look at the clock." 5 a.m. "Oh no, you looked at the clock!" Aaaghgh. It's way too early for this.

Then it began: thoughts of carting children to and from activities this morning and the dishes still sitting in the sink, the Halloween costume I haven't assembled for myself yet, and something hard and crusty on my forehead. Oh, no worries, just pumpkin pulp from the carvings the night before.

There's that itch again. I believe the Holy Spirit comes to us in several ways: maybe by tickle, maybe the memory an old song brings; perhaps opportunities that seem to just fall into our laps. But an itch? Maybe. I'm here aren't I? Now, at 6 a.m. Itch. Itch. The itch I'm currently referring to is of the physical kind today. My lovely garden paid back my neglect by inflicting a hidden vine. One of the poisonous kind. Yes, I have poison "something" on my neck, sides, and now spreading to my arms. I never suspected a thing until the first itch. It crept up on me just like that. And before I recognized it, the rash had already begun to spread.

I've had a nagging thought lately; one that, if I'm not careful, can overtake me. I know this, because I've been here before. The difference today is that I can recognize it; eating away at me, bugging me, even snarling at me sometimes. And in my constant pursuit of holiness (that's my new personal commitment) I'm getting rid of it. Kind of like the unsuspecting vine in my garden; when our conscience is neglected and our thoughts are able to run amok, we can poison ourselves. When one negative thought or emotion is allowed a pass, it can make way for more; eventually it brings us right down to that same level.

There are certainly times when we need to stand up for ourselves, speak the truth, and be heard. And there are times when we can be quiet. Now I'm not saying that God expects us to be doormats for others to emotionally abuse. But I do believe He expects us to achieve self control and discipline, not only in our actions or our words but in our thoughts as well. Don't even let those negative thoughts creep in.

Picture walking through your garden as something tugs at your leg. You force yourself to keep walking, shaking off the thing that tries to hold you back. The tug gets stronger and stronger until you can no longer take another step forward. The tugging is a poisonous vine, wrapping around your ankle, intent on overtaking you. Now imagine pushing that vine down, squashing it; stomping it out. So it is with the garden of our souls. Not letting those negative thoughts take hold of us and control us. We can pray for strength to push the thoughts away. We can pray to recognize the "itch" before it spreads.

So maybe the Holy Spirit did come to me this morning in the form of an itch. I needed to let go, and I have. Thank you, Lord!

And now to take care of my physical itch. I'm about crawling out of my skin! The house is still, thankfully, quiet. The dog is still snoring. The husband is still snoring, too! A fresh pot of coffee is brewing, and my soul is free once again.

Now for the Halloween costume. Maybe I'll go as a zombie mom. That's believable!

Dear God, You are the Master Gardener of my soul. Thank You for Your tender weeding. Thank You for speaking to me in the ways I understand. Please bless all the souls who trust in Your care and love them. Amen.

"In order to discover the character of a people, we have only to observe what they love."

St. Augustine of Hippo

"Rejoice always. Pray without ceasing. In all circumstances give thanks, for this is the will of God for you in Christ Jesus."
1 Thessalonians 5:16–18

Mmmmm. Can you smell that? Wood burning stove and dried leaves. The wind is a little more gusty and cold than I like, but, as I clear the debris from my garden, it stops me in my tracks. My head tilts back almost intuitively to the heavens, and I close my eyes. Inhaling deeply, I take in the autumn air. It is fragrant and reminiscent of my days as a child. The days when my brother and I would rake leaves and pile them at the bottom of the hill at the church next door. We'd run up the hill and roll down into the abyss of debris. Always fun! Those were the days. I am thankful for those memories.

Now my children enjoy that same activity. My husband spent quite some time raking the leaves and neatly piling them in the yard. As he went to the garage to retrieve the leaf blower to suck them up, the kids jumped and spread the leaves all over the front yard. The look on his face when he rounded the corner was predictable, but I laughed in spite of it. He just shrugged and walked away. What a good daddy! I am thankful to have him.

I recently spent the weekend with one of my dearest and sweetest friends; a number of them, actually. This particular friend inspires me constantly to be a good mother, a good friend and is the epitome of a faithful Christian. She has helped me to strengthen my faith in ways I can only begin to express and hope to continue to share with her as our journey as friends continues. I am thankful for her love and friendship.

This time of year as we embark on the Thanksgiving holiday, it is quite easy to go around the dinner table after saying grace and express what we may be thankful for. But how often do we express our thankfulness otherwise? Surely there's always something to be thankful for. Today I make a vow that before I breathe or utter a complaint I will be thankful for at least two other blessings in my life. My hope is that by the time I get to that complaint, I realize that I am truly blessed and it's not necessary or appropriate to complain or whine. Is there really time for that? If we believe in living in the moment of Christ's love and we believe in the gift of faith He has so lovingly given to us and sacrificed for, we can surely accept this gift with gratitude and give our thanks.

For this I pray. And I pray often; to accept the gift and live up to my potential as a loving Christian woman; one who shows mercy and lives in the light; one who is thankful and kind; one who is generous in time and spirit.

So another season has passed. My trowel is put away for the winter. My pots are neatly stored in the garage along with the wind chimes and fertilizer. The Deer Be Gone is also stored and will be ready to defend my garden in the spring. I am thankful for the time spent at my garden table listening to the birds sing me good morning. I am thankful for the beautiful blooms that graced my garden. I am almost thankful for the deer, if for no other reason than inspiring me to write about them!

I am most thankful to our Heavenly Father for yet another day filled with love and the opportunity to share that love with my dearest friends and family. May you be blessed today and everyday with all the goodness He has to offer. Accept His gift with arms stretched. Smile from the inside out!

*L*ord, I thank You for all that You are and all You continue to be in my life. I will thank You and praise You in my thoughts and in my words and in all that I do. I come before You, knees bent, welcoming You. *A*men.

"What is the mark of a love for God? To keep His commandments for the sake of His glory." St. Basil the Great

---

"May the God of endurance and encouragement grant you to think in harmony with one another, in keeping with Christ Jesus, that with one accord you may with one voice glorify the God and Father of our Lord Jesus Christ." Romans 15:5–6

*G*ood morning! Praise the Lord for a beautiful, sunny day! I am just returning from a fantastic weekend with all of my favorite people. And lest I forget to mention, my husband and I brought home a head cold too. Nothing some good rest won't cure. Do you know where to find some?!

Let me set the stage for this story: dishes piled on either side of the sink, I blow the bangs away from my eyes, and I pull up my arm sleeves by biting at the fabric. The dishwater is warm and soapy and almost rejuvenating, if it weren't for the dirty dishes swimming in there! As I wash what can't fit into the dishwasher, I am taken back to memories caught in the photographs outlining the counter tops. Days riding bike with my brother, a warm beach day with my daughter, and crazy hair days with the twins rolling around with sippy cups spilling milk everywhere. Where has the time gone?

I sneeze. And from seemingly nowhere a "God Bless You" comes from below. My little buddy has been sitting at my feet the entire time. He asks, "Are you sick, Mommy?" With a tired nod, I confirm. "I'll be right back!" he assures me.

Holding a baby medicine syringe filled with "potion" he tries to convince me that this will make me feel better. It is a clear solution and I ask, "What is it and where did this come

from?" He looks up at me with those big brown eyes he gets from his Daddy and simply points and says, "from over there." Hmmm. Well, "over there" are lots of different places to make and receive "potion." To name a few: a sink, a toilet, and a bathtub. I was aiming for more clarity on where exactly this came from, but all I got was, "trust me, Momma." So I took the plunge. I drank his little syringe of boy-made medicine. It tasted like water. That's all I'll say about that. He smiled and giggled and moved on.

I guess we just never know what moments are going to stick with us or those around us. How we use our loveliness or not can have a great impact. All of this takes a great amount of patience at times; especially when we are weak, tired, sick, and completely at the bottom of our own barrel.

How wonderful to know that God is there for us. He finishes the race. He dries our eyes. He puts the extra wind in our sails. He brings us grace when there isn't any left for us to give. And He forgives us when we are less than beautiful.

Dear God, it's me again! Knocking on Your door. Thank You for all that we are and all that we hope to become. Bless all Your people wherever they may be on their personal journey in finding rest in You. I love You, Lord!   Amen.

"As sailors are guided by a star to the port, so Christians are guided to heaven by Mary."   St. Thomas Aquinas

"Where can I hide from Your Spirit? From Your presence, where can I flee? If I ascend to the heavens, You are there; if I lie down in Sheol, You are there too. If I fly with the wings of dawn and alight beyond the sea, even there Your hand will guide me, Your right hand hold me fast." Psalms 139:7–10

Lay me down in green pastures and let the wind sweep over my body like the warm breath of Jesus. The sun is high in the sky today. I have goose bumps from the rays kissing my skin.

You might call them God-bumps even. Taking in a deep breath, I become one with the ground on which I lie. It is so peaceful and quiet. In my mind I see flowers swaying back and forth, green leaves bursting from swollen buds. Annoyed, I feel a tickle on my leg jerking me to consciousness. Nothing but a little old ant.

Sitting up now, peering over the great expanse of this empty hillside, I wonder if this is how the shepherds sat so long ago while they watched over their sheep that night. The night the star appeared. Did they know that something so routine as watching their flock would become such a night to remember? Did they know that they were precisely where they were meant to be? Did they know the Savior was to be born? Something, someone, awesome was about to change their lives forever.

I am in preparation mode for our Savior's birth. I look forward to December all year long. I get the house all decorated with greenery and lights. The holiday music plays in the background without ceasing. Sugar plums dance in our heads every night as we hope and pray that this year will be more special than the last. But I wonder if we are truly ready. Are we ready in our hearts to receive Jesus? Are we really celebrating the true reason for this Christmas season? For how can we celebrate Christmas without celebrating Jesus? Christmas is more than just the decorations and the music. It is a chance to celebrate the coming of our Savior. It is a time for a new beginning. It is a time for tradition. It is a time for love and a time for family. And it is a time for giving thanks. Thank you, God, for sending us your Son! Thank you, Mary, for accepting God's call to be not only Jesus' mother, but the mother of us all. We rejoice in Jesus' name as we pray:

Dearest Father, again we thank You for sending us Your Son, Our Savior. Thank You for thinking that we are so worthy of such a gift. We pray that our hearts and our minds receive Jesus and the gift of His life for all that it is. Please bless us and watch over us. Remind us that the Spirit is the reason for this joyous Holiday. In Your name we honor and praise You.

Amen.

"Behold the power of the Virgin Mother: She wounded and took captive the heart of God."

St. Bernardino of Siena

"Mary said, 'Behold, I am the handmaid of the Lord. May it be done to me according to Your Word.' Then the angel departed from her." Luke 1:38

We are on day two of a fever in our house. One of my twins is home from school again today. I am a bit under myself and was looking forward to some quiet in the house and a break from being the "nurse." But it is an honorable job and one that I really do cherish. I couldn't help this morning, though, to take her temperature three different times at varying intervals just to see if it was going to go down. I thought to myself, "She must be putting it under a lamp or running it under hot water when I'm not looking. She just wants to stay home and play and snuggle." Who wouldn't? I have to say that I am a pretty good caretaker. Perhaps if I made things around here a little rougher, they wouldn't be so eager to hang out. But then what kind of mother would I be. Certainly not like Mary.

I lay awake thinking about Mary and her visit from the archangel Gabriel. I think I was even dreaming about her and I know I woke up with her on my mind. Imagining myself as a young bride-to-be and falling asleep envisioning my new life and what was to be and then being awakened, not by the creeks of the loud furnace vents and not by the dog snoring next to me, but from the vision of an angel. My pulse races and my mind tries to catch up with the many thoughts that would be racing through my head, "Am I seeing things? Is this really happening to me?" Startled, frightened maybe, I hide under the covers. I also imagine a calming peace washing over me as I strain to hear what Gabriel is telling me.

The bible says that Mary was "perplexed" and wondered what this visit might mean. Gabriel was quick to reassure her and to calm her fears. He said, "Do not be afraid, Mary. You have found favor with God." He goes on to explain that the Holy Spirit will come upon her and she will give birth to the Son of God. To which Mary replies in Luke 1:38, "I am the Lord's servant. May it be done to me as you have said."

Now imagine trying to explain that one! I have had to come up with some good ones in my day, and I don't know how I would explain this to my husband! "No, really! An angel came to me last night and the Holy Spirit has found me with child." Hmmm. This also says a lot about Joseph, Mary's soon to be husband. The faith and commitment they had with God is unfathomable and, might I say, incomparable to anything I've experienced. I commit, though, to trying.

Today I am looking, as I do many days, to our dear Holy Mother Mary for guidance. I am looking to her for patience and I am thinking ever so fondly of her devotion to our Lord as her child. When we can't be with our own mothers or when we need advice or someone just to talk to, Mary is there for us, too. She is the first mother of us all.

Taking care of my sick kiddo this morning has turned into a morning I will remember fondly. We spent time together reading her journal. She shared with me a fantastically, magical story she is writing about a vegetarian dragon who can't remember how to breathe fire. This time with her, nursing her and snuggling, has provided us the opportunity to connect in a way I didn't even realize existed. Seems she is a budding writer in addition to being an animal care and rescue enthusiast.

While I await the TheraFlu tea to kick in, head still pounding, breakfast dishes waiting in the sink, Mackenzie needs a drink and the dog is whining to go outside. My treadmill has cobwebs on it and Lord only knows what is to come this afternoon. The list gets longer by the minute. But what does it all matter? I have spent time with the Lord today, and it can only get better from here!

Many blessings to you today.

Father, thank You for yet another opportunity to share Your joy. Thank You for this day. Thank You for Mary, a true mother to model. Amen.

"Only after the Last Judgment will Mary get any rest; from now until then, she is much too busy with her children."

St. John Vianney

"May God be gracious to us and bless us, may God's face shine upon us." Psalms 67:2

I've been watching those old Christmas movies again. The movies where 'what can go wrong does' crack me up the most, especially where strands of lights and Christmas trees are concerned. I can relate well.

One fine, fall afternoon, I recruited my children to help decorate the outside of the house with Christmas lights. I thought I'd be smart and spare myself the numb fingertips and frozen, dripping nose. It was unusually warm that Sunday: 80 degrees, I'd say; my husband disagrees, but we know who was right! Either way, I was short sleeved and having a ball! Quite honestly, it was one of the most precious days spent with those kids. They were so excited: singing Christmas songs, pretending to be sledding down the hill. We twisted lights around every stump, bush, and tree we could find. In the end, a jumbled mess of extension cords strung from one end of the yard to the other. Now for the moment we'd worked so hard for! 3, 2, 1: Lights on! Well, almost.

Generally, we wait until at least Thanksgiving has passed before we employ the lighting show, but of course we needed to make sure it was all in working order. And it was. Every tree lit up beautifully, showing our Christmas spirit in an array of bright holiday colors. We even had some blinkers!

Upon returning from the weekend out of town, the kids turned on the outside lights. The left side of the house stood a little darker than I'd recalled. "Hmmm. I thought I put lights over there. Weren't there some blinking lights on that far bush?" It was too late to investigate. "I'll check it out tomorrow," I reassured the kids.

And so tomorrow came. It turned out there was a gap in the strand. One bush was covered with lights and a cord dangling. Then a tree with only lights on the trunk and three bare bushes. And then two bushes with lights and a cord dangling. "I've been robbed!" I tried to imagine someone actually approaching my home and unwinding lights from my trees and then running off laughing. Then it hit me. The deer! They can't eat my flowers, so they are thieving away with my lights! I searched the property for a string of rove lights. I was hopeful of finding a wrangled deer—caught in my headlights. No luck. I still don't know what happened to those lights. In any event, I made do with what I had and reconnected and added more.

Now the final presentation of lights. I got smart this year, too, in another way. I added timers for convenience and to save me from the bitter encounter I face daily to plug them all in. OK, right on time. I heard the click and saw the beautiful lights twinkling in the branches. A candy-cane striped tree welcomed visitors at the drive. Blue and green graced the walkway and multicolored lights shimmered in the low bushes. My, what a fine job we've done. And then "click." Darkness. GRRR. The fuse blew. Again and again and again. Seems the surge was too much for my pitiful house. So I jimmied it up real good and out smarted it. We were lit like the Fourth of July, and couldn't have been happier!

Today I had an angel visit me. Well, kind of. He was the refrigerator repair man. It wasn't because he fixed the fridge either that I call him an angel. It's because of what he said to me as he was leaving. He said very simply, "Thanks. God bless you. Have a very Merry Christmas." I was actually caught by surprise. Had I said or done something that let him know it was "OK" to say this to me? Had he seen a sign in my home that led him to believe and feel comfortable as if he was with a friend? I responded with a quiet, "Thank you" and, "You, too." Then we had a brief conversation about being blessed with the gift of our faith. He told me that he couldn't imagine ever going at this life alone and that we are called to be a witness every moment of our lives. It was clear to me that I probably didn't do or say anything to encourage this blessing. This man lives his faith and professes and shares as he is called to do. An angel.

*O*h Lord, You are the most high and we praise You. Your face shines on us with all glory. May we feel called to share Your love and Your joy with those we encounter; be the friend or friends we don't know yet. Help us to wear our faith on our sleeves for all to see. Help me, Lord, to always be able and joyful to share my love for You. May I not shy away from offering others blessings in words or actions. I hold You above all.

Amen.

"All truth, wherever it is found, belongs to us as Christians."
St. Justin Martyr

"... and his mother kept all these things in her heart." Luke 2:51

I held her hand a little tighter and nuzzled her closer than usual. I could feel my heart breaking as if her sadness was being transfused through me by the warmth of her smaller hand inside of mine. No one saw our pain. We masked it underneath smiles. Leaving the party that she was not invited to, but having left her twin who was, we fought the cold December wind as it bit our cheeks and urged us to scurry to the warm vehicle awaiting.
As she did the "click-it or ticket" behind me, my forehead fell to the steering wheel in a quiet thud. And I sobbed. Tears rolled down my cheeks. My heart literally sank to my stomach. This child of mine who remained with me had yet again been passed up. She said hello to common friends and said good bye to them, too, as she was one of a few who wasn't invited to celebrate. Asking me why, yet again, she is so invisible; I have no answer. Only tears for her. I weep at the memory of seeing her brown eyes looking at me with a half smile on her face. She shrugged and replied, perhaps to herself, "Maybe someday."

When my child cries, I cry. When she is hurt, I am hurt. And it won't go away. I write with tear-swollen eyes. The pain in my heart for her is very real. My bottom lip still quivers when I recount that night.

I spent some time last evening in the company of some beautiful women at a candlelight service. The image of Jesus holding my child close and caring for her is a blessing I took home with me. I am realizing that I cannot be my daughter's savior. She has one already and that Jesus loves her even more than I do. And when I can't care for her and fix things, I can see

Jesus holding her closely; cupping her small face in his hands and filling her heart and soul with a loving peace.

Perhaps there will be a day when she gives witness to Christ's love through sharing the crosses she bears as a child. Or perhaps these moments will become just a faint, distant memory for her. I do know that it's not all for nothing. There is a great plan for her and I know she is cared for. I won't ever stop hurting with my children, whether they know it or not. I will continue to pray for them, knowing that their Father loves them and is caring for them. And I will treasure all these things in my heart.

Dear God, please watch out for my sweet children. Be their loving Father, especially when they need You the most. Please bless their hearts and souls with Your kindness and love. Be at their side always, holding their hand when they need a friend and carrying them when they need a Father. I am truly thankful for Your love in my life. I am thankful for the teachings of Your Spirit and I am thankful for the life You've given me. Please bless me as a mother, a wife, a friend, and as Your daughter. *Amen.*

"You, who have the kingdom of heaven, are not a poor little woman, but a queen."
St. Jordan of Saxony

"And Simeon blessed them and said to Mary, His mother, 'Behold, this child is destined for the fall and the rise of many in Israel, and to be a sign that will be contradicted (and you yourself a sword will pierce) so that the thoughts of many hearts may be revealed.'" Luke 2:34–35

I don't know about you, but I have been running around in a flurry the past few days. The laundry's been thrown on the bed, toys are piling on the stairs, dishes are walking themselves to the dishwasher, and the dust bunnies are setting up a small colony under my hutch. Oh, they're harmless enough, I just don't particularly like them.

While running the vacuum and dusting the dining room table, all at the same time, I stopped to pick something up off of the floor. Bending over, something caught my eye from the dining room window. I switched the vacuum to off and wiped my brow. It was then that I heard one of my favorite songs playing on the music station. Mesmerized by the flakes floating to the ground from seemingly nowhere, the song sent me back in time. All was quiet as I just listened and watched fluffs of cotton fall.

I never really knew it was a holiday song, but since it's on the holiday station I guess it is. I am put in another place when I hear it. I can't explain it. Maybe it's the piano and the horn, the soft voice, the words. Auld Lang Syne means "the good old days." Perhaps that's what stops me in my tracks and hypnotizes me. I think back about friendships that are no more, for one reason or another. Memories of laughing and crying with "old" best friends come back to me. Things I've long forgotten about. In the end of the song, the two have nothing left to say, and they go their separate ways. Back to their lives, probably happy to have seen each other but left with a sadness. That's how it appears to me, anyway. I am left feeling blessed that I have memories of good times in the first place and feel very content and happy with where I am now. The knowledge that everything happens for a reason and that we can't change the past, only live in the present and look forward to the future, makes me hopeful.

Relocating to different cities and new homes over the past several years has made me a little stubborn about making new friends. It takes a great deal of effort and emotion. I have thought for a long time now that I don't need anyone new. My old ones are great! Irreplaceable. But sometimes having a friend close enough to hug is a necessity. Having a friend who lets you come in and sit at the kitchen table and drink half-caf out of snowmen coffee cups and cry about your kids is priceless. These are new memories being created; ones that I am reminded of when an old familiar song plays. And I smile.

"So that the thoughts of many hearts will be revealed." Isn't that the truth? It sounds like a love story. When I read this my own heart skipped a beat and I couldn't help but say, "Amen!" with my hand clenching my chest. Isn't that what we all want? Those thoughts that lie deep within our hearts that are either too dark or scary to utter and of those dreams buried under to-do lists a mile long; those are the thoughts that only He hears. I close my eyes and sink into my soul, as I know only He knows me the best. And also to know that He was sent to us by our Heavenly Father to be our Savior, our friend. I'm overwhelmed with emotion and gratitude at the immense love that He has for us.

Though time may change the relationships we have here in this life, there is no changing or replacing the friendship and deep, sincere love Jesus has for us. We can have our ups and downs in our journey, but He's always there. He knows the thoughts in our hearts that our lips may never speak. And for that I am thankful.

Dearest Father, thank You for Your Son. Thank You for a lifetime of memories and good friends. *A*men.

"God does not ask for our blood, but for our faith."

St. Cyprian of Carthage

"For, 'All flesh is like grass, and all its glory like the flower of the field; the grass withers and the flower wilts, but the Word of the Lord remains forever.'" 1 Peter 1:24–25

All that remains of my fair garden is the dead, limp foliage. Once so strong and vibrant, it now has little to offer in this winter carnage. And although the leaves have long died, cutting back now will only stunt the future growth of these beauties in the spring. So I leave it alone, waiting for a blustery wind to eventually tug at them just enough to be swept away.

From my perch in the window I spy the empty bird feeders. The deer have eaten the seeds again. I can only use my imagination now to recall where the garden lies. Under faded mulch and dead leaves, the precious bulbs await in sleep for the warm spring and summer days. I, too, am waiting for the sweet, precious warm days. I am not a good winter person. I wouldn't mind taking a long nap, too, only to wake up on a sunny day, bursting with beauty, well rested and ready to share my splendor. But I am not a flower bulb, just a mom and a wife and a blessed child of God.

Have you ever found yourself praying for something over and over and never seeing your prayer answered? We've all been there. Even when you plead, bargain, cry and whine when you don't get your way. Frustrating, isn't it? Well, I got to thinking about this one the other day. I was having a conversation with God while driving to flag football. We were in our home away from home: the minivan. As I pelted a cheeseburger (only ketchup, please) to someone in the backseat, I asked God to please get these kids to stop fighting and arguing. "Tell them to be quiet! Just make them sit still for 20 minutes! All I want is some quiet!" I felt like my requests were evaporating as fast as I was saying them. And then it hit me. Perhaps I wasn't praying about the right things. I was praying out of selfishness. My intentions were only to gain some peace and quiet for myself. Not too much to ask, really. (See, I'm doing it again!) Then I started to think about what my prayers are not. They aren't so that my children will learn a better way to communicate with each other. They weren't about bringing love and friendship into the moment. They weren't Godly prayers. If it isn't for God, it isn't worth doing or saying. So I'm trying that new approach to praying. In addition to being thankful, I'm trying to find the God moment in every moment. This goes beyond the crazy kids in the back seat. It's about illnesses, death, financial failure, relationship issues and so much more.

How can I learn and grow in the moments most painful to me if I can't see God in those same moments? If I can't, there is something wrong with how I'm thinking. This New Year's, in addition to expanding my garden, the one that boasts summer blooms and the garden of my soul, I resolve to better praying. I intend to not only be more purposeful in my prayers, but to accept God's will as the answer to them. I vow to quiet my own complaining and whining, thus being able to hear His gentle whispering, calling me to follow Him in the way a faithful disciple does.

Dear God, it's me again. I want You to know that I am trying. I am thankful for Your love. I'm sorry I was cranky today. I will do better tomorrow. You always give me such joy and fill the darkness that sometimes lies in my heart. You know the weight of the feelings I bear inside. I can't hide from You. You are everlasting. You are forever.   *A*men.

"Faith is the ear of the soul."   St. Clement of Alexandria

"But as it is written: 'What eye has not seen, and ear has not heard, and what has not entered the human heart, what God has prepared for those who love him.'" 1 Corinthians 2:9

*A*nd there were three.

I've heard it said that God doesn't give us any more than we can handle. I believe it, I really do. Giving up my worries and concerns and fear is difficult for me at times.

Do you ever feel as though everything you work to achieve every day is all in preparation for something bigger? As if the preparation is equipping you with the tools you may need someday to fight a battle and come out on top? As if working your faith life, growing closer to God each day through the mass, the sacraments, prayer and thanksgiving, is building a stronger you to not only make it to the next life with our Heavenly Father, but to also make it through this life.

Suffering with anxiety, worry, fear, restlessness and distractions of the internal kind are hard enough on adults; we can self medicate, self help, pray, and seek medical attention. But for a child to suffer and not be equipped with the ability to articulate feelings or to even know the difference between what are normal feelings and those which are off just a bit, can be frightening and isolating. Not having the words to describe the loneliness and confusion can be debilitating.

And there were three.

So there came a whisper that urged me to pay closer attention than I normally do. A whisper that urged me to find some help. And in that help, answers were revealed. I did

not breathe a sigh of relief. I was left with more questions and worries than before. But we now have a chance for brighter days.

My husband held me close to his heart and hugged me with the tenderness I needed and allowed me to cry. He doesn't cry on the outside, but I know his heart aches, too. As we held each other close in a silent embrace, a tug on my arm sleeve caused me to pull away slightly. Looking up at me with her precious brown eyes, my daughter nuzzled in between us. And we three stood together, bound by love and a new hope. "It's all going to be OK." I whispered to myself.

God doesn't give us anything we can't handle. His Word, both in scripture and in Christ in the blessed sacrament, is given to us to guide us and to comfort us in our moments of despair and sorrow. I believe that every cross we bear is in preparation for something bigger and something better yet to come. God has prepared mighty things for those who love Him. I have faith. I have love. I have joy.

*D*earest Father, thank You for the moments that bring me to my knees. Thank You for humbling me in Your sight. I ask that You watch over and protect our family. Love us, as we are Your children. *A*men.

"Hope always draws the soul from the beauty that is seen to what is beyond, always kindles the desire for the hidden through what is perceived." St. Gregory of Nyssa

"Just so, every good tree bears good fruit, and a rotten tree bears bad fruit. A good tree cannot bear bad fruit, nor can a rotten tree bear good fruit. Every tree that does not bear good fruit will be cut down and thrown into the fire. So by their fruits you will know them." Matthew 7:17, 20

*T*hese are the days memories are made of.

The Christmas holiday has sputtered to an end. Done are the cookie exchanges as well as the cookies. The presents are unwrapped; little wires and stray pieces of paper and tape stuck to the bottom of my sock remind me. My Christmas tree has shed its needles, revealing dry branches, tired of bearing the weight of lights and ornaments.

Today is a day to remember. While the fire crackles like only gas logs can, the house is unusually quiet. The kids woke up to find a fine blanket of snow covering the ground. In their jammies they scurried to unearth snow pants and mittens, buried beneath shoes and backpacks thrown into the closet before winter break. They knew, certainly, the snow would melt by lunch time. As they raced out the front door, leaving it wide open, of course, I inhaled the cool winter air. The bite of the chill nipped at my cheeks but was refreshing all the same.

I, too, scurried. I rounded up the hot chocolate cups readying them for the invasion of cold cheeks, frostbitten fingertips, and runny noses, which was going to embark on my kitchen shortly.

Filled to the brim, in each little cup was some of the best melted chocolate I've ever tasted. Happily resting on top were gooey marshmallows, with more on the side, of course!

As predicted, the snow licked their tender skin and wind whipped them about. They were no sooner outside when they appeared again at the door.

As they indulged in their chocolate heaven, I peeled off wet clothes, only to place them in the drier and prepare for round two. Six little boots lined the heat register and zippers clinked the inside of the dryer door. From the laundry room I could hear the giggles and the arguing over who made the best snow angel. These are the moments they'll remember.

What moments in life will you remember? Better yet, which moments will you choose to remember? Some of the greatest times in my life have been the simplest. I recall being tucked into bed at night by my mom. She would whisper the story of The Three Bears. Her voice was so soft, yet every syllable was distinct as I would strain to hear the words. Sweet are the memories of my mom playing the piano in the living room as I promised to go to sleep if she played one more song. There are big moments I cherish, too. The day I married my husband, the man I wouldn't dare try to live without. And the days my children were born. They give me the reason to live. And all the special little moments in between and around. Those are worth remembering.

I have chosen to allow Christ to walk with me everywhere I go. If I don't want Him to see it, hear it, experience it, then I'm not going to do it. That's what happens when we invite Him. I want to create and be a part of moments worthy for the King to experience. These are the memories worth making. And how I will be recognized is created in these times. I pray that His greatness exudes everything I do. I pray that the joy which flows through my very being is evident in the way I behave and speak.

As we end another year and look forward to the next, we may be making our list of resolutions. What are you adding to your list? Does it include weight loss, cleaning your closet, becoming more organized? And does it also include filling your basket with the fruits of the Spirit? And taking Jesus along with you every step of the way, building your temple from the inside out? Create memorable moments and be recognized by the good fruit you bear.

Christ Jesus, to You I pray: Thank You for accepting my invitation to walk with me. I ask that You continue to guide me and gently remind me of whom I wish to be when I falter just a bit. Be that soft whisper to quiet me and the loving arms to hold me. *Amen.*

"Those whose hearts are pure are the temples of the Holy Spirit." St. Lucy

"I am the gate. Whoever enters through me will be saved, and will come in and go out and find pasture." John 10:9

The warm days of summer certainly are gone. I realize that Halloween, Thanksgiving, and Christmas should have been a real hint. But it wasn't until just this past week when the temperatures outside dipped into the single digits that I most missed those days; when the only thing that warms me is lying on the hearth of the fireplace like a fat cat. As the warmth of the flames kiss my skin, I'm suddenly taken to my perch at the garden chair. The bubbling fountain in my ear, birds singing me good morning and the hint of dirt and wet grass fills my senses. The twinkling of my wind chimes, which bears a little sign that says, "Bless this home," enchants me. My heart exhales.

Where, oh, where does the time go? I miss the succulent aroma of the iris. I miss the warm breeze that hugs me like an old friend. I even miss the stinky stuff I use to keep the deer away. Seeing the snow-covered debris in my garden makes me long for dirty fingernails. Fireflies and ghost stories around the campfire are a distant memory, too.

Reminiscing on the summer that has past, I had no idea what this winter season had in store for me. Certainly there were things I expected to encounter: being very busy during the holidays, not sending out Christmas cards on time (I tried. . . well, kind of), a messy house, and gaining several pounds from too many indulgences. There were other things I didn't really expect: very cold weather (for me anyway) and snow, which is actually a nice treat. There have also been some more personal and emotional struggles that I did not see on the horizon; none of which define me but are certainly a challenge.

Looking back and looking too far ahead are not offering me much solace. I can't change anything that's already happened, and it's nearly impossible to predict what will. Living in the moment feels like the right place to be. We don't know what tomorrow will bring, nor do we even know what the next breath will mean.

The memories are nice. I hope I enjoyed the moment at that time. I think I did. Just as now, I need to enjoy where I am in this moment. I am grateful for the opportunity to bring Jesus along with me. I've grown deeper in my love and faith for Him this past year. I've taken Him along for many rides. "Daughter, your faith has healed you. Go in peace." Luke 9:14

I pray that you find special moments that take your breath away, and in those moments you see the face of Jesus Christ

Himself. I pray that you feel Him loving you and through your faith I pray that you are healed.

Father in Heaven, I fall in love all over again when I read Your Word and receive the sacraments of Your Church. You never stop teaching me about who I am: Your daughter. With faith and love for You, I am healed.   Amen.

"Christ has made my soul beautiful with the jewels of grace and virtue. I belong to Him whom the angels serve."   St. Agnes

---

"In these last days, He spoke to us through a Son, whom He made heir of all things and through Whom He created the universe." Hebrews 1:2

I felt like I was at the end of my emotional rope today. Please tell me that I'm not the only person who's ever been there. If it's you, say Amen.

I can roll from one thing to another, usually without stumbling. I clean the house and pick up messes. I referee squabbles and make lunch while chewing gum at the same time. However, I do have a breaking point, and that point had been reached sooner, rather than later, today.

Maybe it's because I'm sick. Maybe I'm tired. Maybe it's a snow day that I didn't have planned on my calendar and I am feeling sorry for myself that I can't accomplish all of the things on my to-do list.

I tried to find my happy place. I cranked my favorite 80's tunes. I even danced a little. And there it was. I saw the Light at the end of the tunnel. It was calling to me; almost shouting. It was abundantly clear that if I were to deny it any longer, my bible was going to walk over and hit me on the head. The answers were right there in front of me. I have been blinded today.

The kids were quieted with a movie and a snack while I sat in my favorite blue chair. I had my best friend by my side with the words He so lovingly gave us in my hands. For His yoke is light and today my burden is heavy. I knew then, that it was going to be OK.

I opened to the book of Hebrews. The author is unknown, and many of the letters talk about the greatness of Jesus Christ and the importance of His being. It proclaims that Jesus is greater than the angels, greater than Moses, and greater than any high priest or covenant.

Hebrews 1:5 says, "For to which of the angels did God ever say, 'You are my Son; today I have become your Father'? or again, 'I will be his Father and He will be my Son.'"

To paraphrase several versus regarding Moses, it is known that Moses was a most faithful servant to the house of God. Hebrews 3:6 says "But Christ is faithful as a son over God's house. And we are his house, if we hold on to our courage and the hope of which we boast."

God made His Son a little lower than the angels, yet crowned Him with glory and put everything under His feet. It was through His suffering and dying and tasting of death by which we receive His glory. It is through Christ's suffering during temptation that He is able to help us when we are tempted.

I found a lot of comfort and hope in my readings today. Christ is greater than the angels, greater than Moses, even; yet He was made man to experience our flesh so as to be the ultimate God over everything. His humility and suffering was so great. All for us.

This snow day has about come to an end. The hats and mittens have been in and out of the dryer at least three times now. Snow angels cover the front lawn, and as the sun disappears, a fine mist of snow blows past the window. Hot chocolate once again simmers on the stove and the marshmallows are near.

God bless you today as you find your happy place within His Word, His Son, His Church.

*D*earest Lord, thank You for Your sacrifice, for Your life and for Your death. Thank You for being my sweet retreat when my day hasn't gone the way I'd like it to. I love living in Your house, and I will serve it faithfully. *Amen.*

"Understanding is the reward of faith. Therefore, don't seek to understand so that you may believe, but believe so that you may understand."
St. Augustine of Hippo

"I sought the Lord, who answered me, delivered me from all my fears. Look to God that you may be radiant with joy; and your faces may not blush for shame." Psalms 34:5–6

*K*ids are precious aren't they? They can also be relentless in pursuing our attention and very persuasive in their arguments, especially when they throw your own words back in your face or remind you of promises you've made. How's that for gratitude?

My little boy, very quietly and very much "down to business," put one boot on at a time. He tucked his jammie pants into each cuff. Gloves went on his little hands, and he swung open the front door. I just watched from the entryway, admiring how well he did it all by himself. And then he left. He was quite entertaining as I watched him from the dining room window race back and forth on the sidewalk with his new Big Wheel. He was absolutely impervious to the single-digit temperature outside. The wind blushed his cheeks within minutes and made his eyes water. The gloves had been thrown to the side because apparently, "It's hard to steer with those things on!" I stood corrected.

Content that he was safe and having fun, I returned to cleaning and whatever else keeps me busy, when the door bell rang; over and over and over. And there he was: Snotty nose pressed firmly to the glass, he beckoned me to come closer. The wind that whipped through the entry way was bitterly cold. I hugged my sweater tight against me. Those sweet brown eyes stared up at me and that bottom lip was about to quiver as he reminded me that just the night before I had promised to come outside with him and watch him ride. "But you pinky promised, Mom." He cried. And to that I choked out a really bad excuse, "That was before I knew how cold it was." I know, lame. I could see it all over his face that he felt the same way. Wow, did I miss it that time.

I've been thinking about resolutions lately. So far I have not begun any of them; working out, losing weight, cleaning my closet . . . I have great excuses for all of those. But listening to God's whispers is a resolution I have begun. I have heard Him calling me in some most wonderful directions lately. He is calling me to creativity and a desire to grow deeper in faith and in understanding that faith, too. He has called me to pursue health and happiness for my family. The greatest blessing has not only been that I've heard His whispering, but that I've made myself available to listen.

We don't know when or why God calls us to service. Take, for example, Paul. I was reading a magnificent book the other night. It was full of mystery and intrigue; heartache, sadness and hope. It was the book of Acts. Page after page, I was glued to my bible. I sat in amazement of the enormous grace Jesus showed to Paul. I was in awe, because, as you may know, Paul was the key persecutor of Jesus Christ. Even as Paul stood there, still breathing murder and ravaging churches and tearing apart families, a great light flashed and a sound only audible to Paul spoke to him. It was the voice of Jesus. He asked Paul why he was persecuting Him. He then told him to go forth and wait for further instruction.

Who can be met by a vision, especially that from the Lord, and not be changed, not be affected? It is said that Paul became unable to speak and, although his eyes were wide open, he could see nothing. He did not eat or drink for three days.

It was this vision that sparked a conversion in Paul. Paul was later to be imprisoned for preaching the Good News. He did not falter in his faith nor his zeal to proclaim Jesus Christ as the Savior.

This story gives me hope. If Jesus could convert the heart of Paul, someone who so personally betrayed Him, then surely He could convert me. Surely, if God can come to Paul and speak to him, He can come and speak to me and to you.

I've been speechless at times; caught up in my own world, thinking about what I'm willing and able to sacrifice in order to become a better disciple. In that haze, God calls to me in a whisper, "I will come to you, all in good time." And when He does, I will walk through that door. So I am readying myself. I am resolving this year to practice self control in my thoughts, words, and actions. I am committing myself to more time reading my bible to find the story God has written for me. And I'm resolving to practice what I've learned. I pinky promise!

Dearest Father in Heaven, I am ready for Your calling. I am ready to walk through the doors You open. I ask that You be gentle in Your requests and lovingly guide my every step.
Amen.

"The virtuous soul that is alone and without a master is like a lone burning coal; it will grow colder rather than hotter."
St. John of the Cross

Dear God,

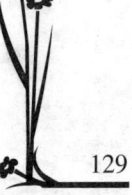

Dearest Father,

Dear Lord,

Heavenly Father,

Dearest Lord,

Father,

About the Author

Christine Schmidt was born Christine Therese Fisher to Raymond Fisher and Karen Dunn. She is the oldest of three children. Born and raised Catholic, it was in a small town in Wisconsin where Christine developed and began cultivating her deep seeded Christian values.

Christine is married to Derek and is the proud mother of four beautiful children. At her home parish, Ascension Church, in Chesterfield, Missouri, Christine actively participates in various women's ministries including Christ Renews His Parish and WINGS: Women In God's Service. It is through her faith and hunger to see God in every moment that she is encouraged to help others see Him as well.

"Thought provoking scripture, poignant quotes, and beautifully vivid imagery fill each page and reach out to the heart of every woman who strives to know Christ and live her faith in her every day roles.

Christine realizes and joyfully articulates what it means to journey through life with our Lord at our side.

The reader will recognize herself on every page, through every joy and challenge the author so bravely shares. This book provides comfort and inspiration to our common experiences and a deep appreciation for the extraordinary gifts found hidden within the moments of our ordinary life."

Kathleen Schurter, wife and mother
Director of W.I.N.G.S. (Women in God's Service), Ascension Parish, Chesterfield MO

"Sometimes God's word & His great saints can seem so far away. Christine Schmidt has delineated a close to the heart look at both. A most rich & pleasurable indulgence of sensation, thought & experience awaits the reader in *Strengthening Our Faith One Moment At A Time*. Open & enjoy"

Linda Bock, M.D.
Child & Adolescent Psychiatrist, St. Louis, Missouri